Fallacies in the Allied Nations' Historical Perception as Observed by a British Journalist

Henry Scott Stokes

Hamilton Books

An Imprint of
Rowman & Littlefield
Lanham • Boulder • New York • Toronto • Plymouth, UK

Hamilton Books
4501 Forbes Boulevard, Suite 200, Lanham, Maryland 20706
Hamilton Books Acquisitions Department (301) 459-3366

Unit A, Whitacre Mews, 26-34 Stannary Street,
London SE11 4AB, United Kingdom

Library of Congress Control Number: 2016907749
ISBN: 978-0-7618-6809-5 (pbk : alk. paper)—ISBN: 978-0-7618-6810-1 (electronic)

The book was first published in Japan in Japanese by Shodensha Co. ltd., in 2013.

∞™ The paper used in this publication meets the minimum requirements of American
National Standard for Information Sciences Permanence of Paper for Printed Library
Materials, ANSI/NISO Z39.48-1992.

Contents

Foreword

By Hideaki Kase

Henry Scott Stokes and I have been close friends for many years.

In 1964 Stokes was named the first Tokyo bureau chief of *The Financial Times*, the UK's most distinguished British international business daily; he was only 26 at the time.

Known for his skillful journalism, Stokes was persuaded to become the Tokyo bureau chief of another British daily, *The Times*, in 1967. By 1978 he had moved to *The New York Times*, which he served not only as Tokyo bureau chief, but also as a reporter covering all of Asia.

His friendship with Mishima Yukio brought him into the international spotlight. Shortly before Mishima committed *seppuku*, or ritual suicide, he penned a letter to Stokes.

There is an institution in Tokyo called the FCCJ (Foreign Correspondents' Club of Japan). Nearly 200 foreign journalists belong to the FCC. Stokes is two years my junior, but he is now the FCCJ's most senior member.

Readers will, I am certain, find the author's observations eye-opening. I too learned a great deal from them.

The relationship between England, Stokes' native land, and the US is a close-knit one. However, readers will surely be surprised by the huge gulf between mainstream Japanese and British perceptions of the US.

Stokes recalls how shocked he was, as a small boy standing at the roadside, at the sight of an American tank unit passing through Glastonbury, his hometown.

> These young boys from Idaho, or Utah, or Arkansas or wherever they came from, acted like kings. I still remember the smiles those American kids had on their faces. They were in control. They could do what they well pleased (see Chapter One).

v

> Meeting with the US military for the first time, I had the very powerful feeling, a strong instinct, that these US forces were taking control of our country, not the Germans whom we were supposed to be fighting. The US was a dominant force in our country, which was deeply uncomfortable (see Chapter One).

Like me, Stokes is favorably disposed toward the US. But unlike the English, pro-American Japanese are not made viscerally uncomfortable by the presence of American military bases on our soil, because we have entrusted our national security to US military might.

At some point we stopped taking pride in being Japanese.

I was astounded at my realization that it was the illusion of a "pacifist Constitution," which took control of the Japanese during the postwar era, that caused our awareness of Japan as an independent nation to diminish. Japan remains occupied by the Americans, at least psychologically. We are like drug addicts who can't kick the habit.

March 10, 2013 marked the 67th anniversary of the firebombing of Tokyo.

That night Tokyo Skytree was illuminated with white lights to honor the victims of the air raids. And in Sumida Ward a group of concerned citizens staged a performance intended to draw attention to the terrible tragedy.

Inspired by the group's conscientiousness, Stokes demonstrated his support by writing an introduction to the performance and distributing it to foreign journalists in Tokyo.

Stokes writes about having seen, at a young age, a "dark red glow in the sky" when out walking one evening in Glastonbury. He was looking at the night sky over Bristol, miles away, which had been bombed by the Germans. In this book, Stokes writes that the "dark red clouds over Tokyo during the firebombing raids in WWII must have been on a scale a hundred times greater. Though what I saw that night pales in comparison, it stands with me today as a memory of those years" (Chapter One, p. 12).

He has also handed down judgment on the Tokyo Trials. He has denounced the tribunal, angrily, calling it the epitome of *injustice*.

> The victors must be judged. Fairness, virtue, protocol, and principle, which Western nations have always respected, were ignored in order to continue this performance, which was not worthy of its name (the Tokyo Trials). The spirit of fair play was degraded. Such deception was consistent. That was the truth of the Tokyo Trials. Western civilization had acted in a most uncivilized way. Justice was not done. It was a horrible, pathetic, evil event that took place (see Chapter Three).

Stokes concludes that it is the victors who must be judged.

Within the precincts of Yasukuni Shrine is a copper bust of Dr. Radhabinod Pal, who is well known in Japan as the only justice of the Tokyo Trials to hand down a dissenting judgment.[1] Justice Pal recommended that all defendants be acquitted of all charges. For some reason, both Dr. Pal and his judgment are virtually unknown in the Western world.

Nevertheless, even without Justice Pal, it is likely that the belief that the Tokyo Trials were immensely unjust would have become widespread in Japan.

In his discussion of the Tokyo Trials, Stokes makes no mention of Justice Pal. This causes me to wonder, especially since Stokes is extremely critical of the tribunal.

But even in the absence of Dr. Pal's dissenting judgment, it should be patently obvious that the tribunal was a miscarriage of justice motivated solely by the desire for revenge.

At that kangaroo court Japan was adjudged an aggressor nation. Nevertheless, in the midst of the Tokyo Trials, the armies of Great Britain, France and the Netherlands were engaging in a war of aggression, the intent being to reclaim their former colonies, colonies that Japan had liberated.

Awakened by the example set by Japan, the peoples of Asia rose up and fought valiantly to preserve their independence. This fact alone bears witness to the monumental unfairness of the tribunal.

Stokes argues that the victor nations' historical view with respect to World War II is a mockery of history, and that Japan was not an aggressor nation. On the contrary, Japan was the "light of hope of Asia."[2]

Furthermore, he is certain that Japan has been the victim of baseless accusations concerning the alleged Nanking Massacre and the coercion of military prostitutes (comfort women).

I am often invited to speak abroad, and have noticed that there is very little accurate information about the Nanking "massacre" or the comfort women emanating from Japan. To make matters worse, some of Japan's textbooks include material that supports the aforementioned accusations. This combination of circumstances compounds the difficulty of persuading foreigners that the accusations are false.

According to Stokes, the historical perspective embraced by the victor nations arises from the conviction on the part of Caucasians that they are superior and that persons of color are, therefore, inferior. He wonders why the majority of Japanese subscribe to that historical perspective.

The white race looked down on people of color, perceiving them as subhuman, until Japan upset Western supremacy during World War II, paving the way for the liberation of the Asian and African peoples.

That condescension was truly reprehensible. Soon after Truman dropped atomic bombs on Hiroshima and Nagasaki, he was quoted as saying to Cabinet members, with a smile on his face, "When you have to deal with a beast you have to treat him as a beast." This attitude was not peculiar to Truman; it is shared by the great majority of Europeans and Americans.

Stokes indicates that Japan liberated Asia, and the resulting tidal wave swept over the African continent, ultimately engendering the racial equality that we enjoy today. Japan's involvement in World War II resulted in the dawning of an entirely new era of human history.

After they hear him speak, people who attend Stokes' lectures, which take him all over Japan, often make comments like "I have seen the light!" and "My perception of myself as a Japanese has changed."

It is my hope that the majority of readers will find that their distorted historical perspective, forced on them by the victor nations, will be corrected after they have finished this book. May it receive the wide audience it deserves.

NOTES

1. Radhabinod Pal, International Military Tribunal for the Far East: Dissentient Judgement of Justice Pal (Tokyo: Kokusho-Kankokai, 1999); http://www.sdh-fact.com/CL02_1/65_S4 .pdf.

2. http://www.sdh-fact.com/CL02_1/94_S4.pdf.

Introduction

It was 1964, the year the Summer Olympics were held in Tokyo, when I first set foot on Japanese soil as the first Tokyo bureau chief for *The Financial Times*. I have now been in Japan for 50 years, and am the oldest member of the FCCJ (Foreign Correspondents' Club of Japan).

Growing up in England, I was told time and time again that the Japanese are a barbaric, cruel race. This sort of propaganda is similar to what the Japanese were hearing then: "Death to the *kichiku Bei'ei*, the American and British monsters!"

World War II ended, but British hostility toward Japan did not diminish. It only grew stronger. After all, Japan was responsible for Great Britain's losing every one of its Asian colonies. Raised in that environment, I suppose it was only natural that I too should grow up disliking Japan.

When I first arrived in Japan I never doubted for a moment that Japan had committed war crimes, as adjudged by the Tokyo Trials. I was also convinced that the Japanese had perpetrated a massacre in Nanking.

But the longer I stayed in Japan, the more I learned about 20th-century Japanese and Asian history. At some point I found myself analyzing the past century's events not from an Allied or a Japanese standpoint, but from a third-party perspective. I realized that the opinions I had previously embraced were wrong. My friendship with Mishima Yukio was extremely influential during that process.

In the Greater East Asian War, Japan was fighting for its survival. Gen. Douglas MacArthur said as much in a speech he delivered before the US Congress after the conflict had ended. The Tokyo Trials were a total sham, serving only as a theater for unlawful retribution. And as for the "Nanking Massacre," there is not one shred of evidence attesting to it. However, the Chinese are hell-bent on using foreign journalists and corporations to spread their propaganda throughout the world. There is no point in even debating the comfort women issue.

I find it very disappointing that so few Japanese attempt to discredit the false accusations and set the record straight. In today's international community those who maintain that there was no massacre in Nanking are shunned. They are filed in the same pigeonhole as the Holocaust deniers. This is regrettable, but it is the reality we face. Therefore, we must be prudent. But unless the Japanese state their case and restate it, again and again, these false accusations will go down in history as fact. Japanese efforts in this direction have been pitifully inadequate.

There is no need for the Japanese to be overly considerate or adulatory. It is enough for them to state Japan's position, and let the Americans and the Chinese state their positions. Of course there will be disagreement. There is no way to avoid disagreement; that is the way the world works. If the Japanese adopt an empathetic stance, they will be taken advantage of immediately.

There is one more thing I would like to mention—something that I cannot emphasize enough. That is that most of the instigators at the root of the thorny issues Japan faces now (Nanking, Yasukuni Shrine, comfort women, etc.) vis-à-vis China and Korea, are *Japanese nationals*. It is up to the Japanese to decide how to deal with this particular problem.

The Japanese have yet to extricate themselves from the curse of the victor nations' historical perspective forced on them by the Allies. I will be grateful if this book serves in any way to help them break free.

Henry Scott Stokes
November 25, 2013

Chapter One

US Army Tanks in England, My Homeland

WWII: AN EVENT IN A FARAWAY WORLD

I was born on June 15, 1938. On December 13 of the previous year, Nanking, then capital of the KMT[1] government, fell to the Japanese Army. I was in my mother's womb at the time of the Fall of Nanking. I am a "Nanking baby," timing-wise, so I feel a mystic fate has prompted me to write this book.

My dear father, Harry Scott-Stokes, was playing cricket that afternoon. He was so excited when driving home that he ran his car into a ditch, into a big hole. He was not seriously injured. At least that was the story told within our family.

I grew up in luscious, beautiful rural England. This was pure English countryside, five hours away from London, to the west, by car. All this was the reality in the UK. The country was at peace. Meanwhile, shortly before I was born, war had burst out in China between China and Japan. So there was this very great contrast between the two worlds of England (especially rural England) and China and, at the same time, Japan as well. And from 1937 (that is to say, a year before I was born) onward, horrendous conflict occurred on the Asian continent.

I was a tiny baby looked after by eight females in my home. Those eight ladies were my five sisters, my mother, a nanny, and a housekeeper. My dear father was away during the war. He was serving in the War Office in London much of the time. So I found myself on my own with those adoring ladies. I was very much spoiled. I was so dearly looked after. That is the flaw in my character: I had it too good as a tiny human being. And I always expect things to go well. I'm cheerful and optimistic, even when others are in despair. I always think that a good solution can be found to any problem.

1

That optimism I inherited essentially from my parents, but my sisters were very important too.

My first steps in education were taken at a very small kindergarten run by a lady named Ms. Osborne Smith. It was about two miles away from my home, but countryside security was 100%. We had no problems there. My mother happily sent me off to walk alone through the little town, a very small market town where I was born called Glastonbury. When my younger sister, Charity (who was closest to me in my family, and still is even today), reached the age of three or so, she and I attended kindergarten together. I walked with her through the town, up the little hill, to Ms. Osborne Smith's. It was such a peaceful, quiet, delicious place. When I think of it now, I am filled with nostalgia. I wish I could have offered my dear son, Harry, now age 28, the same gloriously relaxing atmosphere we had at home.

My dear father was managing director of a local business in the shoe trade employing about 500 people, but he was much more than that. He was a brilliant individual who had won a scholarship to high school (a boarding school, Winchester). He had also won a scholarship to Oxford, and had served in India for four years in the British Army. He was fully competent to perform in very different areas of business. In the service he specialized in military finance; he attained the rank of captain. He was also well known in academic circles. He used to show visitors around our town, which had a population of 5,000 people. It's still about the same today. He used to take them to visit the local attraction, which is a historic site in Glastonbury, Somerset—a beautiful, old abbey. That abbey has a history of 800 years or more. My dad was a great expert on that place. He knew a lot about Glastonbury Abbey, as it is called. When we had visitors, as we often did, he would take them on a little tour of the huge site. Today an oak tree, I think, is planted there for my father and there is a little inscription on a memorial plaque saying it was planted in recognition of my dad, whose name was Harry Scott-Stokes, the same as my son.

The rhythm of the days was very quiet. We were not hard-pressed. I took pride in holding my sister Charity by her hand and taking her to kindergarten.

One day a tremendous surprise was in store for us. My memories of that day are vivid. It was June 1944. As anybody who knows English history will recognize, June 1944 was the month in which the so-called Allies, Britain and the United States (mainly the US) mounted an invasion force to enter continental Europe and get past the German defenses on the coast of France. These forces were being lined up exactly in the quiet, unbelievably gentle atmosphere of Glastonbury, the town in which I grew up. They weren't stopping in the town. They were driving through on their way to the south coast of the UK. They would be shipped across to Normandy for the attack on occupied France.

All of this was happening, of course, unbeknownst to me and to many English people. It was a wide security blanket. A security net surrounded the operation. We didn't know very much of what was going on. We did know that the German Army was in retreat in the face of Russian forces, fighting in their own country. We knew that in Asia there was a fierce battle between Japan, on one hand, and the UK and the US, on the other. We knew that was going a little bit better from the Allied point of view. But through all of this, extreme war-consciousness had actually narrowed our daily lives. In many different ways, our lives had already been affected by the war that was raging mainly in France, and in occupied China and in India and, if you like, world-wide.

In other words, we were being made aware, we very small Brits (I was still six years old), that conflicts were raging and that the outcome was uncertain. It was a time when the little things in life were being rationed. We had, I recall, no supplies of items like butter or sugar. Such staple items of the family diet were being denied us. As a child, I wanted sweets. I still have a taste for chocolate. And I wanted milk. We lived in the middle of a dairy paradise. Our home was surrounded by cows and sheep. I used to say to people that the population of sheep and cows in our town exceeded that of human beings. It was very rural, as I previously mentioned.

SHOCK AT THE SIGHT OF AMERICAN TANKS

That day an enormous event took place. That is the shock I just mentioned. And it happened this way: I was walking to the kindergarten with Charity, holding her hand. I was six, she was four. As we walked through the streets, there was a sound of what seemed to be thunder when we were halfway to the kindergarten. I couldn't figure it out. It was a sound I'd never heard. There was a clattering of metal striking something and a rumble. Something was coming around the bend in the road, but we didn't know what it could possibly be. Some kind of unknown vehicle. In fact, it was a tank.

As it came in sight with others coming behind, the thundering noise grew louder and louder. Whose tank was this? On the body of the tank in question was a big white star, as I recall, and that big white star belonged to the US Army. And there were more of them. One after another, more and more came in sight, something like six or ten of them. I got the impression that they might fire on us or anybody. We had no idea of their mission, which would be to invade Europe.

This huge sound got larger and larger, louder and louder, and at that point, we just stopped walking and stood there, two tiny children, looking at this monstrosity with utter surprise. Standing in the turrets of the tanks, that is, on top of the gun turrets, were these very young soldiers, Americans. They had a completely different atmosphere about them. They were so different from the British soldiers we saw. I faced them, and one of these young drivers, probably the first one, waved his hands in the air. He waved his hands and said something like, "Hi!" We didn't know what to say. He threw something small at us. We didn't know what it was, but went to pick it up. Actually, this was my first opportunity to see and hold in my hand a piece of chewing gum. They were offering us free chewing gum in return for just standing there.

That was not pleasing to me as a little boy. Or at least, I felt ambivalence. Today, my feelings toward Americans are just the same as they were then. I was made very uneasy by their use and deployment of weapons. I was not comfortable with that. When I saw that tank for the first time, I thought these people were so much more powerful than anyone else. They must be totally in control of their world. It must be impossible to resist them. Why? Because of their smiles. They were so comfortable with us. British soldiers, British tank forces would never have thrown packets of chewing gum at little children standing in the street. It wasn't part of our lives.

Now, this was a chance encounter, because it happened only once. This chance encounter came at a time when the atmosphere around us was changing very quickly.

One night, walking with my sisters, we saw to the north, where the city of Bristol was, a dark red glow in the sky as we walked down the hill to my house. So I said to my older sisters who were with me, "What is that? What is that glow?" They said, "The Germans are bombing Bristol. The city is on fire." I couldn't believe it. Why would they do that? (Of course, I had little understanding of the meaning of what I was seeing. The dark red clouds over Tokyo during the firebombing raids in WWII must have been on a scale a hundred times greater. Though what I saw that night pales in comparison, it stands with me today as a memory of those years.)

Meeting with the US military for the first time, I had the very powerful feeling, a strong instinct, that these US forces were taking control of our country, not the Germans whom we were supposed to be fighting. The US was a dominant force in our country, which was deeply uncomfortable.

These young boys from Idaho, or Utah, or Arkansas or wherever they came from, acted like kings. I still remember the smiles those American kids had on their faces. They were in control. They could do what they well pleased.

THE DAY I LEARNED
AMERICA HAD TAKEN CONTROL OVER ENGLAND

I wasn't anti-America. Or to put it like this, there were things I loved about the country as a small boy. I loved cowboy stories. I wanted to hear everything about cowboys and Indians, but I knew our country was much older than that. And I probably knew enough history to be aware that the United States had declared its own independence in 1776, and that the Americans didn't need Britain anymore. They wanted their own space. And they wanted our space as well.

And nobody could say no to them. At that time, military expenditure in the world as a whole was already 50% American. Colossal force. And I didn't know the details, but the reality of the security situation was so powerful that even this tiny child could pick up the vibes and know that essentially the UK, Britain, my country had reached its end as an independent force.

Today we had news that Mrs. Thatcher died in England. She fought a little war in the Falkland Islands early in her premiership. For her to succeed, or the British forces to prevail, she needed tremendous support from the United States. The United States, the Reagan administration, was behind the scenes. They were in control of the situation, because they had total control of military intelligence. It was still an American world. We don't have such an apparatus in the UK today. We actually don't have an aircraft carrier. The United States not only has aircraft carriers, but carrier groups as well. I could feel all of this coming somehow as a tiny child. In June of 1944 I felt that America was going to control the world. I had never read a description by any other English person of what it was like to be invaded, but in fact, we were being invaded and occupied by the US. That was the way I felt.

I have never told this story in my life, because it seemed so insignificant, the perceptions of a tiny child. But I see now that what I witnessed needs to be known, because the transfer of power, the power shift, took place instantaneously. America's military buildup was apparent and visible.

Glastonbury, at least, had over 800 years of history, but no respect was paid and young kids came riding tanks from a country only a little over 150 years old. I even felt the power of the young kids waving from the top of the tanks, as if they were kings. Without anti-tank weapons, humans cannot win over tanks. But at the same time, I felt suspicious of the smiles of those kids.

What did they understand about us? They passed through our town without any knowledge that it is a legendary place with connections to King Arthur. Innocently, they smiled and tossed chewing gum, which symbolizes American culture.

VITAL CHANGE IN ASIA AND JAPAN

In Asia, a completely different situation was observed. What was seen in Asia at that time was a big tide toward Asia for Asians. This is a vital difference from the situation in Europe.

I was mistakenly preoccupied with the idea that Asia at that time was coming under the influence of America, just like Europe. I was not aware that Japan was gaining strength and influence in Asia at an amazingly rapid pace. Up until the outbreak of WWII, Indians themselves thought that it would take another several decades for their country to become independent. The control of the empire was seen to last for some time. The reality, however, turned out that the British Empire lost its "gem" because the Indian people fought for their independence against the empire. The trigger for high hopes for Indian independence, as well as for other Asian colonies, was Japan's victory in the Russo-Japanese War in 1905, especially the sea battle of Tsushima. Japan awakened Asians, and the spirit of independence was fostered in the minds of the Asian people. The role Japan played for Asian independence was vital but, being a mere child back then, I was completely unaware of what was going on in Asia.

I thought the war against Japan ended by the dropping of atomic bombs. I thought that the Japanese had lost everything and that their influence was no more. Things, however, did not turn out that way. It is commonly believed, even now in the world, that Japan committed crimes and was punished accordingly.

We need to thoroughly verify world history again. What happened in Nanking at the end of 1937 is one of them. In international society, anyone who says that the "Nanking Massacre" did not take place will be ignored. The "Nanking Massacre" is a historical fact and nobody wants to debate seriously with deniers of historical facts. Whether Japanese people accept it or not, it is the reality of the world. Common knowledge of the world is that the "Nanking Massacre" took place. Deniers are mentioned only within the context of the crazy propaganda of a "cult" group.

Recently, however, a lot of information became available through the website of the Society for the Dissemination of Historical Fact (SDHF). Thanks to Hiromichi Moteki, the SDHF reports are organized logically with evidence to support their argumentation. They are a reasonable foundation on which to base an intellectual discussion. What happened in Nanking is, in fact, different from what is undoubtedly believed in the world today. It is important that we find out what really happened in Nanking.[2]

Unfortunately, however, differing viewpoints have never been introduced to the world in English. The Japanese Ministry of Foreign Affairs should be explaining Japanese viewpoints in English. The reality is that Japan has merely accepted the views of other countries and never seriously counterargued or stood up for Japanese viewpoints. The so-called Tokyo Trials had a great influence on the reaction of Japan. There must be a lot of external pressure from international society. However, Japan should have stood up and spoken out clearly as a sovereign nation once the Occupation ended and

Japan regained her sovereignty in 1952, including the amendment of the Constitution. Japan still needs such efforts.

As for the Tokyo Trials, they were not worthy of the name. Such was clear to everyone. It is misunderstood that Japan accepted the Tokyo Trials. This mistake must be straightened out. So-called Class-A war criminals, including Hideki Tojo, were sentenced to death by hanging, and Japan accepted the executions. What Japan accepted were "judgements" (plural not singular). It was not at all necessary to accept such an unjust trial.

Ichiro Kiyose was the chief defense attorney; he was also given the responsibility of defending Hideki Tojo. At the beginning of the trial, he questioned the jurisdiction of the court to chief jurist Webb and insisted that there was no legal validity for the trials. Webb responded that he would answer the question later, but he never did until the end of the Tokyo Trials.[3] In any case, all things regarded as historical facts should be re-examined, including the "Nanking Massacre."

JAPAN SHOULD STAND UP AND SPEAK OUT

Japanese conservatives believe that Japan did not wage a war of aggression. Instead, they insist that Japan did not invade, but instead liberated Asian countries (from white colonial rule).

As I am a Briton, I look at things from the British viewpoint. From our viewpoint, apparently Japan came to invade the territory that the British Empire possessed as colonies. Japan invaded the empire, so Japan was an aggressor. The American viewpoint must be quite different. I am not an American, so my view is different from that of Americans. Americans will probably claim that since Japan attacked Hawaii, clearly American territory, Japan started a war of aggression against America.

But there should be a Japanese viewpoint, and it should be proclaimed. For example: Japan did not invade Asian countries but made them independent from Western colonial rule. This is a profound claim based on a different perception of history. That is the perception of history from the Japanese side.

Japan must stand up and express the Japanese viewpoint. Enemy nations such as England and America will absolutely not proclaim such a historical view for Japan. If Japan insists that it was England and America that invaded Asia first, that certainly is a fact of history. Western powers (including England) colonized the world: Asia, Australia, North and South America, and Africa. Americans founded their own country on the "New Continent." We all know, from Western films, how bloody the fight was for native Indians to defend their own land. In Hollywood films, the invaders were on the side of justice, and brought civilization to the indigenous people (who were regarded as uncivilized barbarians). The Tokyo Trials were the same: an American theater of justice. Thus, Japan should also disseminate its historical views to the world, declaring that Japan had a great cause.

From the British point of view, Japan was an extraordinary state which used war as a means to resolve international issues. In this respect, Japan was the worst enemy ever. India, for example, was under British rule as a colony for many hundreds of years, beginning with the establishment of the East India Company. Japan stole the British territory in the nick of time. To the British Empire, Japan was absolutely an invader.

The so-called Spice Islands of Indonesia were instantaneously occupied by Japan. So to the Dutch, Japan was an invader. The Asian colonies owned by Western powers turned Japanese. It was like a game of Othello. The name Indonesia was coined by Hatta and Sukarno, who were both leaders of the Indonesian independence movement. Until it became an independent state, with the help of Japan, the area was known as the Dutch East Indies.

IMAGE OF JAPAN IMPLANTED IN MY CHILDHOOD DAYS

I had to change the ideas I had developed about Japan. After I became a journalist, I had to face the reality of the rise in spirit for independence in Asia during and after WWII. From the British viewpoint, the very cause of that rise in spirit was Japan. So there was massive criticism, during and after WWII, of Japan. The image of Japan and the Japanese was that of barbarity and cruelty, and the Japanese were perceived as beasts or demons.

Turning the tables, to the Japanese, Americans and British were *kichiku*, meaning demons and beasts. So naturally, I developed a biased image of Japan and the Japanese in the midst of massive media reports of "demonic and bestial Japanese." As I grew up, I formed such images about Japan and the Japanese, exposed every day to such media reports.

Day after day, news articles and books were full of criticism about Japan. I learned about atrocities committed against western POWs in internment camps by the Japanese Army since I was eight years old or so, because such were reported every day in the newspapers. At that time, the Tokyo Trials were being held, so media criticism was harsh in the extreme.

I never learned anything anti-Japanese from my parents. My father held some nostalgia towards Japan. He married my mother when he was 25 years old. He had an offer from a university in Nagoya, Japan to be a professor of classical studies (he specialized in Greek and Latin). In the early 1920s, my father told my mother that he would like to go to Nagoya. (He did not spend his entire life in England, as his home town lacked a varied lifestyle.) At that time, diplomatic relations with Japan were good and no one talked about Japanese atrocities. Naturally, my father wanted to take his family to Japan.

My father gave up going to Japan because my grandfather was running his own company and needed a successor. My father demanded to be president and managed to keep the entire company in England. Thus my father stayed and took over my grandfather's business. The reports about Japanese atrocities began after 1945. The media reported on the Bataan Death March and the treatment of POWs at internment camps. Whenever there was a report about Japan, more than enough wicked and cruel images were described.

I entered boarding school in Winchester. We all stayed in a dormitory, and discipline was severe. In 1953 when I was 15 years old, I was shocked when I read the novel entitled *A Bar of Shadow*[4] written by Laurens van der Post.[5] The novel is situated in an internment camp in present-day Malaysia. Japanese Sergeant Hara kills a POW with his Japanese sword. Van der Post was an officer of the British Army; the main character in the novel is a leader of the POWs in the camp. In the trial after the war, he saves Hara's life, saying, "Do we have the right to punish the Japanese by suing them in court?"

In this novel as well, the Japanese were described as brutal. Such was simply the feeling of the British people. We just wanted to justify the thinking that "because the Japanese were so brutal, they must have invaded British colonies, and thus invaded the empire to conquer the peace-loving British people by force."

The Japanese will be angry if Japanese soldiers are described as barbarians and the British soldiers as humane gentlemen. But in the circumstance of criticizing the Japanese, van der Post's question: "Do we have the right to punish the Japanese?" really shocked me.

NOTES

1. Abbreviation of Kuomintang (political party founded by Sun Yat-sen); spelled Guomindang in Pinyin transliteration.

2. JUSTICE: Web Library of Modern Japan History http://www.sdh-fact.com/. "Open Questions to President Hu Jin-tao, " http://www.sdh-fact.com/CL02_3/17_S1.pdf; Moteki Hiromichi, "Why PRC President Cannot Respond to Open Questions, " http://www.sdh-fact.com/CL02_1/62_S4.pdf ; "There was a Battle of Nanking but no 'Nanking Massacre ' (Campaign for the Truth of Nanking), " http://www.sdh-fact.com/CL02_1/112_S4.pdf; Matsumura Toshio, "No Americans Witnessed the Nanjing Massacre," http://www.sdh-fact.com/CL02_1/85_S4.pdf .

3. Kobori Keiichiro, ed., The Tokyo Trials: The Unheard Defense, http://www.sdh-fact.com/CL02_1/66_S4.pdf, pp. 10, 19, 33, etc.

4. http://www.fantasticfiction.co.uk/v/laurens-van-der-post/bar-of-shadow.htm .

5. More information on van der Post can be found at http://www.independent.co.uk/news/obituaries/obituary-sir-laurens-van-der-post-1316507.html.

Chapter Two

Is Japan the Only Country That Committed War Crimes?

CHURCHILL'S NASTY REMARKS TOWARD THE JAPANESE

Recently I had a chance to read the most blatant, disgusting, unacceptable exchanges I had ever come across in 40, 50 years. They were in correspondence between Winston Churchill and his wife.[1] Their descriptions of Japanese people were a thousand miles away from the acceptable range of opinions. In other words, Mr. Churchill wrote something to Mrs. Churchill, and she replied, referring to the Japanese as "yellow [Japanese] lice"—unacceptable language on the part of other British people. Mr. and Mrs. Churchill were engaged in a private conversation. However, they used the language of the gutter to describe the enemy.

Now, maybe in warfare when unexpected things happen, people boil up and speak very emotionally, but this struck me as not the reason for that language. I would say was that it was the colonial experience, as well as annoyance and anger with the Japanese that caused them to use those words where they didn't belong. The empire, referred to as one where the sun never set, enjoyed several centuries of prosperity but, alas, fell instantaneously into the hands of yellow dwarfs in the East and collapsed. That sadness, anger, and revenge prevailed.

When I took my first jobs in the West in the media, I immediately became aware that there were certain people who had served in WWII and had deep-rooted vengeful anger toward the Japanese people, though they might never disclose details. My *Financial Times* editor in chief, Gordon Newton, for example, sent me to Japan to open the Tokyo Office of *The Financial Times*, his paper. It was a big decision, but he made it quickly. However, I had the feeling that if I looked at his war record, I would find that he (or friends who

11

served with him) had directly experienced combat with the Japanese. The Japanese would likely be targets of their anger and desire for revenge, and they would have the impression that the Japanese are barbarous. Not all British people felt that way, but some did.

And after the war when we were all, in theory, finished and done with WWII, out came a succession of black-and-white movies that were seen in the 1950s. Two examples are Kurosawa's *Seven Samurai* and Ichikawa Kon's extraordinary film, *Nobi* (English title is *Fires of the Plain*). The latter is a story about Japanese soldiers who get stuck in the mountains in the Philippines. We never know where they really are. Looking at these films, we discover people who are just in a class of their own. They are in a distinct category that we have never experienced in 500 years of empire building, 300 years of empire holding, and 200 years of fantastic imperial existence.

We had some tough struggles with Indians who were in control of parts of their country (the India that they hold now). They were pretty difficult to fight with, and people in Northern Pakistan, which is Afghanistan today, were also pretty difficult to fight with. These are in a special category of toughness, but the Japanese by reputation went far beyond that, much further. The Japanese were totally different from peoples who were colonized. They only had to step briefly into the field, and the British Empire collapsed. Our people were absolutely hypnotized by the Japanese advance in Malaya, going south and into Singapore. And our General Percival, as his name was, the commander in Singapore, took one look at the Japanese in combat, "superior training, previous war experience, discipline and morale" (Allen, 188), and surrendered. As a POW, he later said, "I lost because I never had a chance" (Allen, 23).[2]

Summing up, I found that we in the West had difficulty coming to terms with the Japanese phenomenon. I'm speaking as an English person, but also as someone who has tried to understand. When our understanding increases, we can come to terms with this, but some people met misfortune at the hands of the Japanese military coming into their countries. There were very painful stories. Of course, I heard many stories about Japanese POWs who experienced atrocities in British internment. There were some nasty English individuals who lacked a refined sense of conduct.

When I originally came out to the East in 1964, I was married to a young Jewish woman (half Canadian and half Jewish). She had relatives all over East Asia. She's from a Jewish family who has relatives in Hong Kong, Bangkok, Singapore, or Calcutta.

In Singapore I was introduced to my new wife's cousin, Max Lewis. He was a local businessman, a Polish Jew who had moved to East Asia for business. He was in the beverage trade. My recollection is that they made soft drinks. I don't think they made beer. Max was the unofficial head of the foreign business community in Singapore in the 60s.

Max was in Singapore when the Japanese Army came in early 1942. In February, the famous surrender took place. Max was just one of those lovable human beings, a very warm, agreeable, lovely guy. His wife was there with him, as well as some other people from the business.

At some point he took me aside and he said, "Don't misunderstand me." (He knew I felt comfortable in Japan. I was having a great time in Japan as a young man. I was 27 or 28.) "But when the war started, I was a captive of the Japanese forces. I couldn't escape." He must have been in a prison camp. Then he said, "As a result of the treatment I received at the hands of the Japanese, their interrogations, I lost the ability to father a child. So my wife and I reconciled ourselves to the fact that we would never have children, because I can't function as a human being in that way."

At first my wife and I didn't know what he was talking about. This wasn't a story I wanted to hear. I really loved this guy. So when he told me his story about how, as a result of extreme actions, the Japanese had made him impotent, we were devastated. He was in Japanese hands for three years, from 1942 to 1945. He didn't mention any details. Here is a guy who's very successful. After the war, he started a soft-drink business and made massive amounts of money. He was a really tough, successful Jewish businessman. But he and his wife couldn't have children.

JAPAN HELPED ASIAN COUNTRIES ACHIEVE INDEPENDENCE

At that time, I was Tokyo bureau chief of *The Times of London*. In the world of the whites, anger toward Japan prevailed after WWII. It was a vengeful passion. The Japanese style of war was out of this world. Japan was so strong that it wasn't anything like reality. The British instantaneously lost their empire, which had lasted for several hundred years. The British lost not only battles, but also the colonies of the British Empire, which had prospered for centuries. The reality was not acceptable. Its humiliation, disgrace and insult were so strong that it was not easy to let it go. England was invaded and occupied by Normans in 1066. But we did not allow Napoleon and Hitler to invade us. Such was our pride, humiliated by the fact that our empire's colony was invaded not by whites, but by a colored race, the Japanese. For us, the possibility that a colored race would deprive us of our land, and that colored races would establish independent states on our former colonial territory was just unimaginable.

Atomic bombs were dropped on Japan. The tragedy was indescribable. America did not have to drop them at all. As if conducting experiments on human beings, they dropped atomic bombs, a uranium bomb on Hiroshima and then a plutonium one on Nagasaki. Dropping atomic bombs on humanity fulfilled the need to humiliate the enemy. The Japanese had to be destroyed, thoroughly defeated. Justice meted out by the victors was simply window-dressing. The Allied whites were just not satisfied unless they took revenge against the Japanese. This is the truth. The Tokyo Trials were truly a theater of revenge.

Japan was not invaded when the Mongolians attacked her in 1274 and 1281, but was defeated in WWII. The American Army occupied her mainland. The Occupation was a breach of the Potsdam Declaration, which stated that the Allies would "partially occupy" Japan. The Potsdam Declaration demanded unconditional surrender of the Japanese Army. Because it stated that no deviation from its conditions would be allowed, it was a conditional surrender. But once MacArthur disarmed the Japanese forces, the Allies insisted that Japan surrender unconditionally. American Occupation forces remain in Japan, even after almost 70 years.

An invasion takes place when one country uses force to enter into the territory of another. According to this definition, we can acknowledge that Japan invaded the territory of the colonies of the British Empire. But having heard Hideaki Kase's explanation, I learned about Japan's viewpoint and changed my view as well. Japan not only invaded the territory of the British Empire, but also played a vital role, i.e., helped achieve independence for the people of Asia, who suffered under Western colonial rule. Japan invaded and occupied the territories of Western colonies. Then Japanese officers and soldiers, with a sense of mission like that of missionaries, led their fellow Asians to independence.

The Japanese presented a new concept of racial equality to their fellow Asians, and in the nick of time, they made this ideal a reality. Their motivation was totally different from that of colonial rule. The Japanese desired independence for their fellow Asians.

This was a simple reality, not propaganda. Asian people also had a strong passion for independence. Western people need to review the history of the world from this new historical perspective. We do not have viewpoints like these, and have never dared to accept them.

JAPAN'S SIN: RAPING THE WHITES' COLONIES

Was it evil for Japan to have invaded the Asian colonies of Western nations? If invasion was evil, how should the Western powers' invasions of Asia, Africa, Australia, and North and South America be regarded? No Western nation has ever apologized for such invasions. Why is it only the Japanese who have to apologize for invading Western colonies?

In the Tokyo Trials, we closed our eyes to the question of which countries committed acts of invasion, and punished Japan. Why were the Japanese punished? The reason is not that invasion is evil, but that a colored race invaded white territory. It is acceptable for whites to invade colored territory, because in doing so they are civilizing the uncivilized. When inferior colored races invade white territory, they are committing a crime. The latter act is a sin because it goes against God's will.

The Japanese believe that both sides of a conflict are wrong. This is a flexible and effective way of thinking. We Westerners think, however, in terms of black and white. In a debate, for example, either the affirmative side or negative side takes a stand and argues without compromise. We want to decide which of the two is right, affirmative or negative. We do not arrive at conclusions like "both are right" or "both are wrong." According to this way of thinking, if Japan is right, then the Allied side must be wrong. Thus, the Allies tried hard to prove that justice was with them, on their side.

The Tokyo Trials were, from the beginning, a theater of revenge. The tribunal never did justice to Japan. If it had, it would have been doing injustice to the Allies. Not only the sin of civilian massacre, dropping atomic bombs on Hiroshima and Nagasaki and conducting air raids on all major cities in Japan (including the Tokyo Air Raid), but also the misperception of justice that allows the West to repeatedly attack the rest of the world would have become clear. Such an eventuality had to be prevented. That was the standpoint of the Allies at the Tokyo Trials.

My cousins, the Clothiers, were a little aristocratic. They are the sort of English family who have horses and dogs, and love the countryside. They live in a big house and have lovely parties at Christmas and New Year's. And of course I wanted to meet their beautiful daughters. I appeared with my wife, Akiko, for the first time in this society in 1973. Akiko looked so young then, about 12 years old. My father said to me, "You'd better watch out. There's a law against this. You can't abduct children. This could get you in big trouble." My family was very funny about it.

Then I attended one of those parties hosted by the Clothiers. Akiko was not with me, as I remember it, but she was not far away. The Clothiers knew that I now had a girlfriend, or that I was probably going to marry someone who was Japanese. Big deal. How were they going to face up to this? They had to reexamine their feelings. Why? Because a member of the family, an older woman, had been caught by the Japanese in Hong Kong with other relatives. Their business was in Hong Kong, I expect. And they were kept in a civilian camp, not a POW camp. They were held there for three and a half years. Of course, there's no place to escape to in Hong Kong. There were no books; there weren't enough blankets. There were shortages of everything. But at least they weren't dying. They were survivors. The Clothier cousins came up to me and said, "We are so pleased to know that you have a new member of our family." They added, "We want you to know that we are not opposing your feelings for the young lady. We respect your decision as your decision. Please know we are touched and that you have our support."

This same lady, or one of the other cousins, told my mother what happened when they were in captivity. They had no toilet paper. Excuse me for mentioning this, but the old lady had difficulty without it. The only paper she had was the Bible. She used its pages as toilet paper. It's not a big tragedy, but it's a colorful detail that shows what the attitudes were in England toward the Japanese.

THE WORST HUMILIATION FOR THE BRITISH:
THE FALL OF SINGAPORE

Officially and militarily, the British people had to radically change their understanding of Japan, as well as of the world. In January 1942, Manila was occupied by the Japanese Army, but this was not a big concern for the British. The biggest concerns were Singapore, Malaya, Burma and India. Once Japan joined WWII, battles in the Asian colonies began. Japan showed unbelievable strength. Japan's strength was shown in the Russo-Japanese War in 1905, but at that time the British hadn't experienced Japan's strength directly. So they did not think Japan was such a threat. The British learned of Japan's strength once Japan started heading south along the Malay peninsula to Singapore.

The most shocking event was the sinking of two battleships, the *Prince of Wales* and the *Repulse*, the pride of the British Royal Navy, within only four hours by a Japanese air attack. Battleships out on the open waters had never been sunk by an air attack. Churchill was First Lord of the Admiralty when he was young. He made the decision to dispatch the British fleet to the Pacific, but no attention was paid to defense of the skies. The pride of the British was in the Navy, not the Army. That pride faced humiliation. The British fleet was unable to fight back against the Japanese attack from the sky. The British faced a serious need to review their own naval power and the military power of the Japanese.

Japan's victory in the Russo-Japanese War showed colored people of the world that the coloreds can defeat the whites. This unprecedented shock spread and coloreds saw their hope in victory. But the Western world was not aware of the relative strength of the Japanese Army (and the relative weakness of the Western powers against the Japanese Army) until WWII. So nobody ever imagined such an event would ever happen.

The British Navy, however, maintained its strength on the sea, but the Army did not enjoy such good fortune. India was the property not of the Indians, but the British. India was part of the British Empire. At least, I was so educated. However the armed forces stationed to protect British India were limited. Suddenly, the Japanese Army landed on the Malay peninsula and a battle of a different dimension had begun. Winston Churchill, then the prime minister, was confounded.

Commander Percival of the Singapore Defense Army was paralyzed from fear. He lost his will to fight, and surrendered on February 15, 1942. Japanese commanders must have been surprised by the weakness of the British force. Armies of the Western powers, such as the Dutch,[3] were stationed all over Asia, but they were almost instantaneously defeated by the Japanese Army. Japan had a military force strong enough to defeat all the Western powers in a very short time, and occupy all the Western colonies in Asia.

However, the occupying forces the Western nations stationed in their colonies were not strong enough to defend the Japanese. For the British Empire, Singapore was of vital interest, next to Hong Kong and Shanghai. The Fall of Singapore symbolized the end of British colonial rule.

PLANET OF THE APES: FILM PLOT BECOMES REALITY

The British Empire collapsed due to the Japanese Army. None of the British people had ever imagined such an eventuality. It was so easy to anticipate the shock and humiliation experienced by the British when they were struck with that reality.

It was shocking that Hitler tried to establish a great German Empire after a series of battles with European nations. Hitler was still a white Christian. So we were able to compare him with us. It was, however, beyond the British frame of thinking that the British Empire, which enjoyed its prosperity within the white civilized world, would fall into the hands of a colored race. It was an event that was simply incomprehensible.

There was a hit film entitled *Planet of the Apes*. What could be comparable to what happened then is that the fictional world in the film turned into reality. Nobody thinks *Planet of the Apes* will turn into reality. It's fictional and it's a world that exists only in film. The event is just imaginary. The apes (colored people) which tried to imitate the humans (Westerners) suddenly rise above the humans. If this turned out to be the reality, the shock would be immeasurable, and we can imagine the extent of the impact. The Japanese exerted such an impact on British nationals. A great impact was felt not only by the British, but also by all of Western civilization.

Compared with the European powers, America was much better informed about Japan. Famous Japanologists, such as Ivan Morris, Donald Keene, and Edward Seidensticker, were all trained by the American Army. They learned the Japanese language at military academies and served as intelligence officers.

In Europe, French culture was influenced by Japan. Japan was able to influence the British to a limited extent. In the 1860s, toward the end of the

Edo era, British diplomat Ernest Satow visited Japan; he went back and forth between the two countries for about 40 years. Historian Nobutoshi Hagiwara, my friend from Oxford University, published 500 articles about Ernest Satow in the *Asahi Shimbun*. He sometimes asked me to correct his English grammar.

In any case, the Anglo-Japanese Alliance was signed in 1902. However, the British commoners in general did not deepen their understanding about Japan, despite the establishment of diplomatic relations between the two countries. The British understanding of Japan was extremely limited.

Today we have many specialists in Japanese studies at Oxford University. We have financial support from the government now, but this was not the case in the past. The level of Japanese studies came up to that of Chinese studies. Oxford has various bodies for Japanese studies, such as the Nissan Institute.

HATE TOWARD JAPAN INTENSIFIED BY IGNORANCE

The British had not been defeated for over several hundred years. Victory after victory took place in battles fought to construct the Empire's colonies. I was taught that the British Army always wins and I simply believed that. I was educated with a pink globe. The world was pink in color and the pink areas were British territories. Once WWII ended, however, the British colonies started to declare independence and the pink world changed to one painted in all different colors.

The British Empire lived by thoroughly exploiting its colonies. Our prosperity was dependent on colonialism. A great contrast can be seen compared with Japanese rule. The Japanese government invested a huge amount of money in Korea and Taiwan. But the British Empire was dependent on their colonies for British prosperity. The empire was supposed to win, but it lost the war against Japan and thereby lost all its territories.

This reminds me of the *Tale of the Heike* and its theme of impermanency. Those who enjoyed prosperity were drowned in its temptation. At last, they surrendered even without fighting. Defense was strong at Singapore, but it was defense against an attack from the sea. All cannons pointed at the sea. The British simply were not prepared for an attack from the land.

Diplomats well informed about Japan, as Ernest Satow was, were rare. Our philosophy has changed, and we are now providing British diplomats with opportunities to acquire a great deal of knowledge about Japan. They first learn the Japanese language in Kamakura for two years. Then they deepen their studies about Japan.

Before WWII, the situation was different. The biggest mistake the British made was abrogating the Anglo-Japanese Alliance. A person like me, who has lived in Japan for half a century, and who has a Japanese wife and raised a child in Japan, is regarded as a professional Japan specialist. These specialists, across the board, insist that the abrogation of the Anglo-Japanese Alliance was a big mistake. Of course, Arthur Waley, a historian who translated the *Tale of Genji*, was active in the 1920s. But there were few Japan specialists in Britain then, and they were not very influential. The British people's eyes were focused on Europe.

The image of Japan after WWII was the worst of all. In France, novelist Marguerite Duras[4] wrote *Hiroshima mon amour* ("Hiroshima my love" in English). It sympathizes with the Japanese and became a focus of attention in 1950s Japan. We had no one like her in England. Pictures of a prisoner-of-war camp drawn by Ronald Searle let the world know about Japan. He drew pictures of life in the camp. Nobody saw such pictures. The British people, including myself, came to believe that the Japanese were not human beings. The Sunday press in England always reported on sensational topics. After WWII, they consistently carried negative articles about the Japanese.

In England, we did not have a Japanese community. This was quite different from America, where many Japanese immigrated. Few Japanese lived in England. Moreover, America faced Japan across the Pacific. In terms of distance, the Americans and the Japanese are far apart. But since there were various problems that impacted both nations, their destinies frequently intersected.

VICTOR NATIONS HAVE NO RIGHT TO JUDGE JAPAN

My view toward Japan changed after the 1950s. Earlier I mentioned *A Bar of Shadow* by van der Post,[5] published in 1953. I was impressed by it, and read it aloud to my friends in school. I thought I needed to learn more about the Japanese, and felt it was not fair to racially discriminate against them.

I also felt we should change our attitude toward the German people after WWII. I felt the same about the Japanese people, but British people felt more hostile toward Japanese than they did toward Germans. Apologies offered by the Germans moved the hearts of the British people. Whenever they had the opportunity, Germans apologized and tried to express their humanity. Such efforts changed the attitude of the British people.

Following the trial that condemned Sgt. Hara to death, British officer John Lawrence confided, "I never saw the good of them [war-trials]. It seemed to me just as wrong for us now to condemn Hara under a law which had never been his, of which he had never even heard, as he and his masters had been to punish and kill us for transgressions of the code of Japan that was not ours."

This British officer was under Sergeant Hara's observation. Van der Post himself had actual experience in a prisoner-of-war camp in Malaya. The person called Hara is not a real person, but the novel itself was inspired by real-life events. Sergeant Hara was the overseer of the camp. On a night with a full moon, he drank and took the prisoners he did not like outside the camp and decapitated them with his Japanese sword. He was charged and sentenced to death by the military court. The British officer appealed his sentence and saved Hara's life.

I was strongly moved by this novel and wanted to tell my friends at the boarding school why I felt so. I still have the same feeling. We were not fair to the Japanese. We were not qualified to punish them.

A nation has the right to go to war. It is the most significant right a nation possesses. I have at home a biography of Van der Post that was written by my boss at *The Financial Times*, D. F. Jones. Van der Post insisted, "He [Sgt. Hara] may have done wrong for the right reasons, but how could it be squared by us now doing right in the wrong way? No punishment I could think of could restore the past, could be more futile and more calculated even to give the discredited past a new lease of life in the present than this sore of uncomprehending and uncomprehended vengeance!"

This book was originally very short. More text was added later, and the book became a little thicker than the first edition. Van der Post was Prince Charles' tutor and highly respected in England.

I felt that the Japanese occupation of the British colonies was a justifiable cause. After the war, we judged their sins as if the victor nations were an almighty God. I felt that there was something wrong in this. I felt that way, in spite of the general feeling of hate towards the Japanese. I felt that way because I read van der Post, and his work became the basis for my thinking.

NOTES

1. Nicholson Baker, Human Smoke: The Beginnings of World War II, the End of Civilization (New York: Simon & Schuster, 2008), p. 459.

2. Allen, Louis. *Singapore, 1941-1942*. London: Frank Cass, 1993. Print.

3. Japanese forces landed on Java on March 1, 1942; the Dutch East Indies Army surrendered on March 9, 1942.

4. For more information on Duras, see http://www.nytimes.com/1991/10/20/magazine/the-life-and-loves-of-marguerite-duras.html.

5. More information on van der Post can be found at http://www.independent.co.uk/news/obituaries/obituary-sir-laurens-van-der-post-1316507.html.

Chapter Three

What Was the Objective of Yukio Mishima's Suicide?

MY LAST DINNER WITH YUKIO

Many times, I have visited the hall where the Tokyo Trials were held. It is in the Ichigaya headquarters of the Defense Ministry. PAC 3 (Patriot) surface-to-air missiles were often installed there in the event that North Korea made good on its threat of a nuclear missile attack. In such a tense atmosphere, I visited the court of the Tokyo Trials again. The trials held there were evil. They were criminal acts.

For victorious nations to unilaterally judge defeated countries is unacceptable. It is an act of revenge for the victors to judge the defeated and to execute officers and their men as war criminals. It's a crime.

I learned about the atmosphere that filled the courtroom at the Tokyo Trials from various people involved in the proceedings. The atmosphere was evil and there was poison in the air. Nastiness surrounded the court and people felt the evil intentions of the prosecutors. Thus, the court was full of horrifying energy. The tribunal, which lasted for several years, was entirely illegal.

I have, for over a half-century, worked in Tokyo. No other Tokyo correspondent of the foreign media has lived and worked in Tokyo longer than me. My mind is always full of things about Japan. One regret I have is that I did not properly master the Japanese language.

Several weeks before Mishima's suicide, I dined with him at the Fontainebleau on the top floor of the Imperial Hotel in Hibiya. It was the last time I met with Yukio. He told me, "Henry, it is no use staying in Japan any longer if you do not try to learn Japanese. Pack your things up and leave for your country." I was so embarrassed about not being able to speak Japanese, but

21

Yukio had spoken to me in his usual straightforward way. So I felt, "He's right."

Currently three of us live together: myself, my wife, and my son Harry. My 60-year-old wife is Japanese; we have been married for over 40 years. My son Harry is well known on both the national NHK and private TV stations, in addition to his capacity as a personality for the FM radio station J-Wave. As my wife and son communicate in Japanese, I live in a perfectly Japanized atmosphere. Thus, I do not lead a life that is segregated from things Japanese. Even now, my family observes my table manners and teaches me the Japanese way. My manners are not so good because I am suffering slightly from Parkinson's disease.

Mishima became a historical figure, and sometimes people ask me how I got to know him. It was the spring of 1968. Two years prior to my initial contact with Yukio, John Roderick, the president of FCCJ (Foreign Correspondents' Club of Japan), invited him for a press conference. John was Tokyo correspondent of the AP and I was the Tokyo Bureau chief of *The Financial Times*. The FCCJ was then located at Babasakimon in front of the Imperial Palace. Though I attended the Yukio Mishima conference, I never tried to shake hands with him. Nor did I ever think of conducting an exclusive interview with him. I was in charge of economic affairs.

MY FIRST IMPRESSION OF YUKIO
IN MY EXCLUSIVE INTERVIEW

Two years later, in 1967, I became Tokyo Bureau chief of *The Times of London*. I represented the world's most prestigious daily newspaper in Japan. It was then that I thought of interviewing the most famous man in Japan, Yukio Mishima. I phoned him at his residence in Magome.

The Tokyo Bureau of *The Times* was on the 7th floor of the *Asahi Shimbun* Building in Yurakucho then. I had one of my three female assistants make the phone call. Yukio had built two houses eight years prior to my phone call, one for his parents and the other for welcoming his young new bride, Yoko. Yukio was aggressively writing his long novel, *Kyoko no ie* (Kyoko's house), to pay for the two houses.

I called him around noon. It was his routine to write all night till 5:00 or 6:00 a.m. every day. Around noon was, in fact, not a good time for anyone to wake him up for a phone call. I did not know such a thing, of course, at the time. Yoko answered the phone. She was Yukio's private secretary. Yoko told Yukio that there was a call from *The Times of London*. Yukio immediately responded, "I will answer," and picked up the phone. I spoke to him in English, "I am Henry Scott-Stokes. I am honored to talk with you." Then Yukio asked me, "Are you Mr. Henry Scott-Stokes of *The Times of Lon-*

don?" in English. Then he added, "It's nice to talk with you," in English again.

Yukio was able to communicate in English. He asked me again, "Are you the Tokyo Bureau chief of *The Times of London*" So I said, "Yes." Then Yukio asked, "What is the purpose of your call?" So I said, "I would like to interview you for an article for *The Times of London*."

With the exception of Emperor Showa, Yukio was the most attention-getting Japanese internationally at that time. Mishima's international recognition was unbeatable. No one had caught up with his fame. Yukio was always straightforward. He always told everyone what he had in mind. His views and opinions were very occasionally inconsistent over a long period of time, but that made him even more attractive. Were I unable to interview Yukio, it would mean that I would miss the opportunity to cover the most talked-about Japanese on earth. Thus, I decided to meet him without deciding on any particular theme on which to base my interview. As a journalist, I was eager to get to know Yukio Mishima. His voice was deep and rough, very intimate, and reminded me of that of a heavy smoker. In fact, Yukio smoked 30 to 40 cigarettes a day. He always carried with him Peace cigarettes (they came in cans) sold by the state bureau, together with his black schedule book. Yukio answered in his deep, low voice, "I am happy to meet with you." I could feel his excitement. I was happy, too.

Yukio designated the Hotel Okura as our meeting place. We decided to meet late one afternoon at a bar in the Okura. As the day to meet Yukio got closer, my three young staff ladies found it difficult to contain their excitement. They were thrilled that their boss, a young foreign reporter, was able to meet the famous Yukio Mishima so easily.

The Orchid Bar was the only bar I knew in the Okura, so I took it for granted that we were to meet there, but Yukio was planning to meet me in the men-only Oak Bar on the mezzanine. On that day I arrived a little early and waited for him at the Orchid Bar, but he did not show up at the appointed time. Thirty minutes later, a hotel clerk solemnly came up to me and asked, "Do you have an appointment with Mr. Yukio Mishima?" He told me that Yukio was waiting for me at the Oak Bar. I rushed there. At the center of the vast bar, I found a small man with big round eyes, all by himself, puffing quickly as if he was irritated. The man spotted me and stared at me with his big eyes. I apologized by saying, "I'm sorry, Mr. Mishima. I went to the wrong bar. It's my mistake." Then Yukio said, "Never mind. What shall we drink?" So I ordered beer. No one else was in the bar except us.

Yukio wanted to talk in a private place where no one would be watching us. He wanted to be interviewed in a place he felt comfortable, where he could speak freely. I was surprised by the fact that he was very short. I noticed that I should not take photos with the two of us standing side by side. I never paid such heed to anyone being short, but with Yukio, I felt that instinctively. Yukio had his own space in which he felt comfortable. I felt that I should not enter his space. Since our first encounter, I started paying attention to the space in which Yukio feels comfortable.

NO LOVE LOST ON JAPAN'S RIGHT WING

International politics was in a critical phase in 1968. It was the year that America's Vietnam War failed. The following year that superpower sent human beings to the moon, but was unable to win a war against a small Asiatic country. That year, 1969, was a turning point, when a shadow was cast over America's overwhelming strength.

It was in this context that I spoke with Yukio regarding the state of the world's political affairs. Japanese media reports were vague. There were many reporters from *The New York Times* who believed that America's war in Vietnam would end miserably. Everywhere in the world, student radicals protested. And in Japan, *Zengakuren*, a group of student radicals united all across the nation, actively protested in public. Only a little after 10 years since the end of WWII, the situation had turned 180 degrees. America, which had held global hegemony, lost a war with a small country in Asia. The world faced a phase of uncertainty.

I visited Vietnam in the summer of 1965. Two years before that, Kennedy was assassinated. Lyndon Johnson, who replaced Kennedy as president and was later elected in his own right to be the president, ordered additional dispatches of troops to Vietnam in 1965. When I entered Vietnam, I was a *Financial Times* reporter. As soon as I went into the war zone, I immediately felt that America would lose. Just like France, America, which invaded Vietnam, did not know anything about Vietnamese society. America continued its air raids, but Americans themselves did not comprehend what they were doing at all.

Yukio sensed that the world was drastically changing. In such an atmosphere, Yukio made up his mind to organize the *Tatenokai* (Shield Society). When I first met him, he had no inkling of how to organize such a group. Yukio told me about Lord Byron, a famous romantic poet and English hero (1788–1824). Lord Byron took his expedition to Greece, defeated Turkey and organized a private militia to fight for Greek independence. Yukio suggested to me that we write a book about Lord Byron together. Yukio said he wanted to know how Byron gathered his soldiers. How did he attract young people and have them join his private militia? Byron created his militia, defeated the Turkish army, and succeeded in acquiring independence for Greece. Yukio wanted to play a similar role in Japan.

It was the fall of 1968 when Yukio secretly organized his private militia, *Tatenokai*. It became publicly known in 1969. It was 1969 when I reported on *Tatenokai* training at the foot of Mt. Fuji. Thinking ahead, Yukio made his approach to the SDF (Self-Defense Forces). He started associating with SDF officers, perhaps, through introductions from Diet member Yasuhiro Naka-sone, who later became Defense Agency chief and prime minister, as well as other conservative Diet members. Both Yukio and Nakasone took advantage of each other. According to Yukio, Nakasone asked him to give a speech at a rally of his supporters in Tokyo while Yukio was staying at Shimoda in Izu. Yukio said he declined the request.

Yukio was losing confidence in politicians. He thought they were useless people. After all, politicians do nothing—they can't do anything. No politi-cian can sacrifice himself for a great cause. Yukio had lost all confidence in them. From Yukio's viewpoint, not one had made up their mind to pledge their life. No politician wanted to rise with Yukio.

Shintaro Ishihara, later a Diet member and governor of Tokyo, was the same. Playboy as he was, he yachted around Aburatsubo, an inlet off the Miura Peninsula. Tall, handsome and attractive, Ishihara was a populist. Yukio expected Ishihara to concentrate on his writing job, but he started appearing on TV and was busily trying to maintain his popularity.

Though Yukio had lost heart, he then started a debate with leftist students of Tokyo University. He could sympathize with leftist students. During his youth, Yukio was influenced by leftist ideas. Someone recommended that he join the Communist Party. It may sound strange, but Yukio was not counting on right-wingers.

MY BYLINE ARTICLE IN *THE TIMES OF LONDON*

Yukio wanted to get young people to join his *Tatenokai* private militia. Hiroshi Mochimaru was precious to him, as Mochimaru was a student at Waseda University and a leader of conservative student activities. He also was an editor of the conservative students' newspaper.

In the spring of 1969, when I went to report on *Tatenokai* training at the foot of Mt. Fuji, Mochimaru made all the preparations for me. I heard that Masahiro Miyazaki, a renowned critic and specialist of China issues, intro-duced Masakatsu Morita, who committed suicide together with Yukio at Ichigaya, to Yukio. Miyazaki was instrumental in convincing a lot of young people to join *Tatenokai*.

On March 17, 1969, *The Times of London* carried my byline article on Yukio Mishima and his training at the foot of Mt. Fuji. At that time, the Japanese media intentionally ignored Yukio's *Tatenokai*. Compared with the huge number of leftist student demonstrations in various places, *Tatenokai* was miniscule. But when we look at what followed, my article on the *Tateno-kai* was forecasting what took place after the training at Mt. Fuji.

The Times—Monday, March 17, 1969
Japan Army trains right-wing group
From HENRY SCOTT-STOKES
Fuji Camp, March 16

The Japanese Army has embarked on a unique training programme for right-wing nationalist students here, in a move which is likely to provoke political controversy.

For the first time since the war, the Army, or Ground Self-Defence Force, as it is called in Japan, is training students, equipping them with rifles, and integrating them into its training programme. The group concerned consists mainly of students and a few graduates in their early twenties, and is led and mainly financed by the Japanese writer Yukio Mishima, the most active right-wing intellectual in Japan.

Last week some 50 members of this group, with Mr. Mishima at their head, were training at the camp on the snow-covered slopes of Mount Fuji in basic fieldcraft and "guerrilla tactics" as Mr. Mishima describes them. They trained with the latest 1964-type Japanese rifle.

All these students are members of Mr. Mishima's Tate No Kai (Shield Society), a kind of private army whose self-proclaimed function is to act as a "national guard" with a responsibility to "protect the Emperor", possibly by taking action against left-wing students in the future.

Tens of thousands of Japanese civilians have stayed for short periods at Japanese army camps since the war, largely because they provide cheap camping holidays and a change of air. Mr. Mishima's group has been afforded quite unusual privileges, however.

No other civilians are permitted to handle firearms in the camps. No other large group is permitted to train for a month at a time. No other group is receiving anything like the concentrated attention and professional care given to the Tate No Kai.

Mr. Mishima prepared the way for training his "army" by negotiations with the Japanese military authorities, especially the Defence Agency, two years ago. The principal concession be sought from the head of the agency at that time was on an agreement to permit Tate No Kai students to handle firearms. After a year of negotiations, the matter was finally agreed, but Tate No Kai members are still not allowed to fire rifles. One striking feature of the Tate No Kai is their splendid khaki and green uniforms, paid for by Mr. Mishima and designed by him.

The whole conception of the Tate No Kai–to form a national guard of sorts with some help from the army—must seem eccentric not only to many Japanese but also to foreigners. This is one reason why there has so far been little reaction here to Mr. Mishima's activities, although they were briefly reported last year.

However, the Tate No Kai should not be dismissed lightly. Its members are small (Mr. Mishima's target is only 100) but they are a most striking group of students in terms of intellect and self-confidence. Only one applicant in 30 has been allowed to join recently.

These students may be compared with the extreme left-wingers of the Sampa Zengakuren. Both groups share the same scorn for Japanese party politics and the same lack of respect for the nation's "peace" constitution, though their creeds are totally opposed.

The small size of the Tate No Kai does not give a true indication of its importance. This and other Japanese nationalist groups, like their prewar predecessors, make up for their small size with their determination to act when called on to do so.

The Tate No Kai has, patently, a narrow ideological foundation. Respect for the Emperor, anti-communism, defence-mindedness, love of traditional culture are values overtly shared by few Japanese youths today. Yet one may still feel that the most powerful undercurrent in Japan today is nationalism, which is historically associated with the right, not left.

Much still depends on Mr. Mishima himself. This stocky, muscular, very successful man commands fantastic personal loyalty amongst his students, "I have committed myself now and will not turn back", he told me at the weekend.[1]

FIVE-YEAR COUNTDOWN TO SUICIDE

Yukio felt he was getting old, year by year. When he first came to the FCCJ, he looked to be in his mid-thirties. But four years later in 1970, he looked to be in his mid-forties. Yukio's two vehicles: *The Sea of Fertility* (*Hojo no umi*), a tetralogy, and *Tatenokai* proceeded simultaneously. He never told anyone about the scenario leading to his death, but I am positive he knew about it. It started with the writing of *The Sea of Fertility*, and was finalized when he finished writing the tetralogy.

When Yukio finished writing *Spring Snow* (*Haru no yuki*), he started his training with the SDF. In 1968 when he finished the second volume, *Runaway Horses* (*Homba*), he organized *Tatenokai*. When he finished the third volume, *The Temple of Dawn* (*Akatsuki no tera*), he selected five members. Those five took part in the Ichigaya incident. The fourth volume, *The Decay of the Angel* (*Tennin gosui*), records November 25, 1970, the day of the incident, as the date of completion of his work.

Actually, he finished writing it in the summer of 1970. Yukio wanted to have Donald Keene read the final volume of *The Sea of Fertility* as quickly as possible. I never asked Yukio about this possible scenario, but there was a pattern. Even if my guess is wrong, it will be a handy tool for a researcher who wishes to understand Yukio's death.

The planning of his suicide required an enormous amount of time, labor, and attention to detail. The act itself was expressed intellectually and in a literary style. It involved a countdown with a five-year duration.

The planning of the suicide may have started in 1964 or 1965. People say that Yukio wouldn't have committed suicide had he had won the Nobel Prize in Literature, but I do not agree. Yukio's purpose was not winning a Nobel Prize. Restoring Japan's essential national entity, or *kokutai*, destroyed by the

Occupation army, was his target. He sought revision of the "illegal" status of the SDF and of the Emperor's unacceptable "declaration of humanity" on New Year's Day of 1946. Yukio thought either a coup d'état or revolutionary means was an acceptable way to destroy Japan's occupied status.

Interestingly enough, whenever I used the expression *uyoku*, or right wing, he always thought that I was referring to *yakuza*, or gangsters. Yukio told me that he had separated himself from their world. In fact, he had no contacts in it. So whenever he was told that a right-winger wanted to see him, he declined the request.

Once a gift was delivered to Yukio's residence in Magome. It was a huge coffin. Yukio was frightened by this. He felt that his life was in jeopardy. For more than a year, he had a police guard around his house. During that time, both Yukio and Yoko had to put up with police security. For Yukio, such behavior and its consequences became synonymous with the *uyoku*.

After Yukio's death, I was invited to tea by the novelist and entrepreneurial owner of the Saison Group of companies, Seiji Tsutsumi. I had never met him before, but he was close to Yukio, so I visited his company. I was led to a Japanese-style *tatami* room by Seiji only to find a small man there who had arrived before me. It was Yoshio Kodama, a big-shot right-wing figure. I am sure Kodama also had some sort of relationship with Yukio.

Neither politicians nor right-wingers had any intention to change occupied Japan by risking their own lives. Yukio sacrificed his life to demonstrate the importance of *kokutai* to society. The reality has yet to change, but at least Yukio took up the challenge. Someone may follow in his footsteps. My mother-in-law told me that today's Japanese are cowards, so it will take another 200 or 300 years.

He chose to live eternally through his death. It's the same with religious martyrs. The difference, however, is that he chose to live such a life for his own sake. The man Yukio Mishima was either saint or devil. Someday I might make a final judgment of my own, that he was a devil. Someday I might think that he was a saint. Or, I might conclude that he was a genius. I myself haven't finalized my evaluation of Yukio Mishima.

MACARTHUR'S ARROGANCE AND INSINCERITY

The Daiichi Life Insurance Building is cater-corner from the building that houses the FCCJ. MacArthur's General Headquarters (GHQ) of the occupation army were in that building, which overlooks the Imperial Palace. MacArthur made everything seem like scenes out of a drama. He was a sick man suffering from selfish pride. GHQ helped him exercise his flair for drama. The Occupation army has been criticized for a variety of reasons. What is unacceptable to me is its arrogance. The UK took the initiative with the

Nuremberg Trials so America would not have a chance to control them. In performing his drama, the Tokyo Trials, MacArthur intended to disseminate American justice to the world, exact retribution against the Japanese, and issue a warning to Asians.

The Foreign Correspondents' Club of Japan was founded when MacArthur occupied Japan. Its purpose was to report to the world how America's occupation of Japan was a just, humane and historical achievement. The FCCJ's banner proudly stated, "Est. 1945," the year Japan was occupied. In other words, the FCCJ was the headquarters for the dissemination of MacArthur's Occupation policies, and the historical view that prevailed at the Tokyo Trials. MacArthur fully utilized the power of the media to beautifully embellish his own ego.

The organization was called the General Headquarters for the Allied Powers. It sounds official but, in reality, GHQ was MacArthur's private possession. His will was everything. He preferred directing, as if he were making a film. Thus, the organization was a projection of MacArthur's ego and of his narcissistic personality.

For the past five years or so, I've been reading about Matthew Perry, who arrived at Uraga, Japan in his so-called Black Ships. In the process, I researched MacArthur and GHQ as a comparison. Some of my research results are in my previous book, *"Why Did the U.S. Wage War Against Japan?"* co-authored with Hideaki Kase, a well-known critic and special advisor to former Prime Ministers Yasuhiro Nakasone and Takeo Fukuda. As for the details, I hope you read my book,[2] but in a nutshell, both Perry and MacArthur craved the limelight, and considered their own performances more important than anything else.

From Occupation policies to the Tokyo Trials, everything was simply a manifestation of MacArthur's own inner character. His arrogance and insincerity were despicable. MacArthur pretended he was a Japanese *shogun*. But unlike a real *shogun*, his authority was virtually almighty. He mistakenly believed he was an earthly god whose mission was to exercise God's will on His behalf. So he acted accordingly: he attempted to control everything under creation, including the Japanese emperor. He behaved as if he were the Creator: he devised Occupation policies without giving any consideration at all to international law.

He tried to disseminate American justice, to show the world how everything should be interpreted and judged. He used his own performance as a yardstick for judgment. The results show a clear contradiction: none of his "justice" could be used as a yardstick. Everything America claimed as her virtues—civilization, justice, fairness—was neglected, nonexistent in MacArthur's occupation of Japan.

Japanese newspapers at that time, including the *Asahi Shimbun,* adored MacArthur, as if he were a living god, and paid their respects accordingly. They tended to worship Hitler, MacArthur and Mao Zedong.

VICTOR NATIONS SHOULD BE JUDGED

What America did during the Occupation was evil, as evil as appalling revenge or lynchings. Complete deception and nonsense persisted thereafter.

MacArthur intended to demonstrate that the white race is superior to all others. The supremacy of Western civilization, which can be traced back to the ancient Greek period, when Plato and Socrates were renowned, must be shown to the small, yellow creatures who lived in uncivilized, barbaric societies. He wanted to show those barbarians what civilization was all about.

All Japanese nationals were accused at the Tokyo Trials. They were supposed to simply accept, without any criticism or opposition whatsoever, the noble wisdom of civilization. That was MacArthur's arrogant message.

Today all facets of Japanese society, including major Japanese newspapers, the Ministry of Science and Education, and schoolteachers, have absorbed the disrespectful attitude of the occupation period. They believe that the Occupation policies were all exceptional, and accept the historical viewpoint forced upon them by the Tokyo Trials. In this respect, MacArthur achieved a great deal. Today's Japan is still MacArthur's Japan.

But the reality is that the events of the tribunal led to Western civilization's being judged. I believe this was the core of the Tokyo Trials. It became more and more clear that it was not Japan, but the victors who should be accused. Contrary to MacArthur's intentions, it was revealed that the prosecutors committed much heavier crimes, one after another, than the accused.

The victors must be judged. Fairness, virtue, protocol, and principle, which Western nations have always respected, were ignored in order to continue this performance, which was not worthy of its name (the Tokyo Trials). The spirit of fair play was degraded. Such deception was consistent. That was the truth of the Tokyo Trials. Western civilization had acted in a most uncivilized way. Justice was not done. It was a horrible, pathetic, evil event that took place. Chief jurist Webb said, after he went back to his home country, Australia, that "the trials were wrong."

I felt dark when we visited the place where the International Military Tribunal for the Far East took place the other day. No Western professor will acknowledge the injustice of the Tokyo Trials. This is extremely critical.

NOTES

1. Scott Stokes, Henry. "Japan Army Trains Right-wing Group." *The Times of London* 15 Mar. 1969.

2. The Road from Perry's Arrival to Pearl Harbor: Why America Started a War Against Japan, http://www.sdh-fact.com/CL02_1/93_S4.pdf.

Chapter Four

Osaka City Mayor Toru Hashimoto's Press Conference and the "Comfort Women" Issue

MAYOR HASHIMOTO'S MISPERCEIVED REMARKS

Osaka Mayor Toru Hashimoto held a press conference here at the Foreign Correspondents' Club of Japan regarding the comfort women issue.[1]

More than 300 correspondents and journalists of the foreign media assembled. The main conference room was full; there was no space left even for standees. Two separate sites were connected with closed-circuit televisions, but those rooms also filled up. The building was absolutely packed on the 20th floor, where the conference rooms were located, as well as the 19th floor. I've never seen so many cameramen, so many human bodies. There was so much demand for space. It was impossible for regular members to get even standing-room tickets. I'd never heard of that before. The stairs going down to the 19th floor were jam-packed with photographers. What pictures could they take in there? They were just waiting for him to appear. This chaotic scene made me think back to the day when Abe-san and other candidates for the LDP leadership met here. This time there were 10 times as many cameramen. Of course all the networks were present, so this was a most concentrated expression of Japanese popular interest in this issue.

Mayor Hashimoto appeared quite uncomfortable. He prepared the text of his speech, printed in both Japanese and in English. He was not his usual energetic self, as seen on news broadcasts. I wouldn't say he seemed disconcerted, but he certainly didn't seem to want to be there. He kept saying, "What I really meant to say was . . . ." Only a very naïve politician would use such words, because someone who says, "What I really meant to say" is actually showing weakness. It is just not really straightforward to say, "what I really meant to say was such-and-such."

As for the question-and-answer session, it went on too long. Mr. Hashimoto makes it his rule to answer questions as long as time permits at press conferences, but this one dragged on and on. Hardly anybody left the meeting, but there was no atmosphere of excitement or even interest. It was like turning up for a gala party, an event, rather than coming to hear someone speak about a significant topic.

What he actually said in his prepared speech was: "It wasn't only Japan that had prostitutes at the front lines; it was more or less a universal affliction." He didn't get that point across by saying, "What I really meant to say was . . . ." I felt very sorry for him.

He's a young man, about half my age, and he was not properly advised. I think he could have expanded the idea that prostitution is the oldest profession in the world, for better or worse. We don't usually refer to that famous statement because it's a cliché. But there you are, that's what he meant.

MY FIRST NIGHT IN TOKYO

When I came here, to Japan, for the first time, I was offered a woman, on just about the first night. In those days a *hodokan* (press officer) from the Gaimusho (Ministry of Foreign Affairs) would take me to a bar in Ginza where women were being served up like dishes of fish. "Would you like *maguro* (tuna)? Or something else, Mr. Stokes?" At that time I was a bureau chief, but I was very young. When I went to my room in the Okura Hotel, I found a woman there whom I had never met before in my life! And, of course, I wasn't paying anything. But I still remember her. As bureau chief of a foreign media company, I worked closely with the *hodokan*. He had sort of pretty hair and looked like a pimp, not like someone from the Gaimusho. I don't remember his name, but perhaps it's better that way. After the 1964 Tokyo Olympics, that practice stopped.

Like providing free cigarettes in reception rooms for businessmen, it used to be absolutely universal. Everybody put cigarettes on the table when they had meetings. That stopped suddenly. And of course, prostitution, again at the time of the Olympics, was banned—in theory. At that time a well-known newspaper owner came to visit me. When he arrived at Haneda Airport, then the main airport, I was horrified to discover he had no secretary. Why was I horrified? Because then I knew I was to be responsible for him. What was he going to want? To go to Ginza bars and indulge his fantasies. I knew this would come up. I absolutely knew. And I had never been in the position of procuring women for men or men for men, or anyone for anybody.

There have been other cases like that of this newspaper owner. Young journalists, especially young foreign correspondents, are constantly tempted. None of this is openly mentioned. There was no awareness of the evolution of the role of comfort women here in Tokyo, within the heart of the government. Nobody mentioned that. So this subject is kind of like a cesspool, a dirty, odious pond. I arrived in Akasaka with this newspaper owner. He was staying at one of the hotels there, I forget which. He said, "Well, let's see. We're gonna go out tonight, Mr. Stokes. Would you mind accompanying me?"

I was thinking about all of these things that happened 40 years ago, when the subject of comfort women came up. In Korea, a lot of people died in the war, and in Vietnam, a country which was torn open by huge wars, prostitution was really big. I think I needed to mention that.

PRESS CONFERENCE ENTRAPS EVEN KAKUEI TANAKA

In Hashimoto's place I would have hoped to avoid getting into this situation. What should he have done to save his skin? How could coming to the FCCJ help him escape? I asked myself those questions as I sat there. I did not have any answers. He was putting his head into a lion's mouth. People here are absolutely pitiless when it comes to politicians who make mistakes. Not holding the press conference could have been one of his options.

I was very close with Kaku-san (former Prime Minister Kakuei Tanaka, who was arrested in connection with a bribery scandal), and with *Oba-chan*, his mother. The first time I met Kaku-san was when he was finance minister. I went to the *Okurasho* (the Ministry of Finance) and met Kaku-san there to do a one-on-one interview. This was arranged by the *Nikkei*. I saw him for the first time in early 1965, when I was *The Financial Times* bureau chief.

The day of the interview, I went to the wrong building. I went to the neighboring *Gaimusho* building. I thought, mistakenly, that he used the same building as the foreign minister. When I arrived at the *Gaimusho*, I was told, "You are in the wrong building. You need to go to the *Okurasho* next door." At that time, interviews by foreign correspondents were very rare, but the *Nikkei* wanted to know what he would say, so they helped me get the interview with him. Kaku-san was a very powerful man.

I went into his office, where he was surrounded by subtle, quick-minded, and very arrogant *Okurasho* bureaucrats. Kaku-san was marvelous, I thought. He had all these *Okurasho* officials under his spell. They meant nothing to him. His approach to the job of minister of finance was to encourage the bureaucrats to speak their minds to him. Usually a minister is less informed about the details, so tends to depend on bureaucrats and follow their recommendations. But Kaku-san was called the "bulldozer with a computer" and he instantaneously came up with numbers, names, and trivial details. He also did calculations—simply off the top of his head—much more quickly than the bureaucrats.

While he was being interviewed by me, sitting there in his chair, he took my business card in his hand. As he talked, he tapped it against his finger-nails. He did not have a disorder. This reflected his energy level, which was tremendously high. He spoke in Japanese, with one of his bureaucrats inter-preting. I didn't bring an interpreter from my office. I knew so little about Japan and Tokyo then.

By that time, he'd held the LDP (Liberal Democratic Party) *kanjicho* (secretary-general) job, and was ready to become prime minister. Later, when he did hold that office, he was extremely popular, and was respected as a modern day *Taiko* (Toyotomi Hideyoshi, who ruled towards the end of the Warring States Period). Like Hideyoshi, he rose to the pinnacle of society, though he did not come from a noble or wealthy family background.

But Tanaka didn't know how the Foreign Correspondents' Club worked. He came to the club, where he was asked questions he hadn't prepared for. He didn't know that the *Bungei Shunju*[2] articles were going to be important. He hadn't the faintest idea.

Shigezo Hayasaka, his press secretary, should have prepared him. (Haya-chan was a friend of mine who also knew many foreign correspondents slightly, but only one or two well.) It would have been even better to resort to the only dignified strategy: cancel the meeting. Hayasaka should have used the argument that he did not want Tanaka to be insulted. He understood that some very hostile questions had been prepared.

Haya-chan should have known about the time former Prime Minister Ichiro Hatoyama came to the Foreign Correspondents' Club in the spring of 1946 for an evening party just before the elections. This episode is in our club records, so there's no doubt about it. When Hatoyama stood up to make a few remarks, he presented a cask of *sake* he had brought with him. This was a Japanese politician's way of saluting the club and being a nice chap. American journalists present interpreted (or chose to interpret) his gesture as an attempt on Hatoyama's part to corrupt them with the *sake*. Then came questions, notably from a Canadian reporter named Mark Gayn. Hayasaka could have canceled the conference; he must have known that questions like Gayn's would be asked. It would have been the right thing to do, because the hostile questions Hatoyama subsequently received caused him to lose face.

The next morning, the Japanese-language newspapers were full of reports describing Hatoyama as an unsuitable candidate. Shortly thereafter, SCAP issued an order banning him from politics for the next six years. Therefore, during the whole of the Occupation, Hatoyama was paralyzed politically. Very few people know this story. Haya-chan himself didn't know it. But if he had asked me what to do with his boss, I hope I would have given him the advice I am giving now. As evidenced by the Hatoyama case, the Foreign Correspondent's Club can be a very dangerous place. Even to top-flight reporters, such as *The New York Times* bureau chief, the prime minister's press secretary should have said, "Look, we want you to dwell deeply on our politics. But this is going too far."

Alas, Haya-chan was so busy that he hadn't had time to consult with me. Also, the attack came from such an unexpected quarter, because at that point, Kaku-san was best known for opening the door to China. The people who were after him were on the right in Japanese politics, and they deeply resented his overtures to China. The extreme right was believed to be a physical threat to Kaku-san, so much so that his residence in Mejiro was always heavily guarded. Mayor Hashimoto should have asked what happened to Kaku-san.

If you asked them today, very few of our members would know what happened to Mr. Hatoyama in the spring of '46. With the death of Samuel Jameson, I am practically the longest-living *gaijin kisha* (foreign correspondent). I am the unelected dean of foreign journalists here. I shouldn't say that, certainly not in a loud voice, but quietly: that is who I am now. A lot of experience is required to be able to come to terms with this. I don't think anybody realizes how much fuss was made over this man's remarks.

Osaka Mayor Hashimoto was very unhappy about the articles written about him, which basically said that, in effect, he despises women, that he thinks very little of them. If he wanted to prove them wrong, he could. For example, he could appear on television shows in Japan with some of the leading women in Japanese society. He could have asked Sakurai-san (renowned female journalist Yoshiko Sakurai), who is my friend as well as his. She's a good lady with name recognition. Just the fact that the two of them appeared side by side would be sufficient. Or they could do a big conference at a hotel. I once did such a conference with Sakurai-san at the Imperial Hotel. We had about 500 people, a huge audience. She and I were on the big stage in the Teikoku (Imperial) Hotel. And it was very lively.

That's what Hashimoto should have done, go to a hotel. It would have been better to organize his supporters. He should not have come here. He was trying to get across to a Japanese audience, to the people of Japan, with this conference. To do that, he should have gone to neutral territory. The Foreign Correspondents' Club is not neutral. He can come here anytime. And intellectually, that would have been more interesting for us. If he had appeared at the Imperial Hotel, I would not be talking about this now. At the FCCJ reporters' remarks create disputes.

HISTORY OF "COMFORT WOMEN" IN BATTLE ZONES

Up to the 18th century there were no massive wars that engulfed the entire European continent. Wars were between limited numbers of people and battles took place in the open, in fields or on mountains, not in cities. The level of destruction was much lower. With the advent of Napoleon, everything changed. We now had wars of massive scale, and the violence spilled over into Asia from Europe. A classic case is the Opium Wars. Let's remember that until the early 1840s, it took the scourge of modern war roughly 50 years after Napoleon to tear our societies apart. Modern warfare, as developed by Napoleon and used against Napoleon, a passionate general, developed as large-scale conflict, engulfing not only entire landscapes, but also whole countries. At this point, civil society was torn apart. Only really strong societies could possibly survive modern warfare without tremendous amounts of distress. And that was most obvious in Europe.

But the situation, the dislocation of societies, was quite well understood. And part of that dislocation, only a small part of it, was prostitution. Women were escorted into battle, as it were. In the old days, the only women escorted into battle were admiring princesses and aristocrats. But the "Helen-of-Troy" concept of warfare, wherein wonderful women attracted glamorous male foreigners from other parts of the world, vanished. Everything became much more sordid, much dirtier. And much cheaper. And much more prevalent. And much more impossible to put an end to. In the old days in Europe, you could say warfare was terminated at a certain point, and it came to an end. Our wars seem limitless. The way things are going, today's conflict in Syria will go on forever. And in Syria today, in Lebanon today, above all in Beirut, might be one of the great centers of modern prostitution, together with Paris, London, and New York. Who is working to limit this trade? This is big business. Is anybody working to end prostitution? Yes, there are volunteer societies. There are people who object to prostitution for health reasons. But essentially, military prostitution is a way of life that took root 200 years ago, and it will never end. So these days, basically as a result of Napoleon, we have to face the fact that warfare has no limit. As soon as war stops in one place, it comes up in another, and this will go on forever. It's one of the miseries of war that women are being exploited in its midst. First of all, you want women in your area wherever you are at war, but you don't want them spreading disease.

How this affected Japan in modern times is that the Japanese were just a bit better organized. Looking back in history, Japan adopted an orderly form of catering to the sexual needs of soldiers on overseas battlefields. So as not to infringe upon the human rights of local women, comfort stations were prepared. The Japanese military set up these establishments to prevent rapes. In this sense it can be said that the Japanese military was far more concerned about the protection of human rights than its counterparts in other countries. We know of cases in history where the spread of sexually transmitted diseases sometimes crippled military operations. Comfort stations made it possible to control sexually transmitted diseases.

So perhaps the role of the so-called comfort women is going to be very prominent as a social issue in the decades to come. I myself have seen with my own eyes what happened in Vietnam, where the streets of Saigon (today Ho Chi Minh City) were full of women for sale. It's the same story in Korea.

When the Americans occupied Japan, their first demand was prostitution facilities for American soldiers. That's the point: the very first thing they asked for. Is this in SCAP[3] records? Yes. Are those SCAP records deeply buried? Yes. There must have been a tug of war going on inside SCAP. On one hand, we had militant Christian groups arguing in favor of aggressive intervention in and interruption of this trade. On the other, we had business interests. What is going on in Macao these days? Or Las Vegas? These are big gambling centers. The basic item for sale is sex. And do we see any chance of this being brought to an end? No, we see, in fact, every indication of it being expanded. How is the Ginza doing these days? Since the Ginza's core commodity is sex, incoming tourists from overseas, from China, Taiwan, and Korea head for the Ginza. And what is foremost in the thoughts of the 25-year old? Sex!

In the days of the Occupation, of course, prostitution was officially highly disapproved of. Exactly how was it organized? The use of comfort women at the US Naval Base in Yokosuka, let's say, should not be overt, so there's no red-light district just outside the front gate of Yokosuka. No, it's a little bit further up the street. Not in front of the buildings, and not on the base. In comes a US ship, full of sailors. Their first dream is to sleep with an Oriental woman. Who is going to deny the existence of prostitution in today's lovely Ginza? It's done very discreetly, very privately, but it's there. There are comfort women for Chinese tourists. This is probably the most active part of the trade.

REBUTTAL EFFECTIVE AGAINST KOREAN CLAIM

Hideaki Kase has done a careful analysis on the subject of comfort women. He has concluded that the Japanese authorities never abducted women. If this is true, which I believe to be broadly the case myself, it is a very important statement. Kase-san continues, "Nor did the authorities force them to become comfort women against their will." This is not to say that comfort women didn't interact with Japanese soldiers. They did.

Kase-san wrote a very insightful piece on this issue[4]. What he pointed out in his essay is the problem of comfort women in Korea after WWII. As a correspondent of UPI, Kase-san visited Korea many times and saw the reality there. His essay, therefore, is very persuasive. He saw advertisements calling for comfort women to service soldiers in the *Dong-a Ilbo* and other leading Korean newspapers. The term "comfort women" (written in the same Chinese characters) was used in those advertisements. In Korean, the expression is pronounced *wianbu* and in Japanese, *ianfu*. *Wianbu* and *ianfu* mean exactly the same thing. Mr. Kase was in Korea the year before diplomatic relations were established between Japan and South Korea.

In his essay he rebuts various arguments regarding the comfort women controversy, which do nothing but heap abuse on Japan. In his rebuttal Kase-san introduces a research report entitled "The Military and Sexual Violence in 20th-Century Korea," compiled by Korean scholars. According to the report, due to the outbreak of the Korean War, comfort women were made available to US officers and soldiers. They were referred to as *yanggongju* (Western princesses), *yanggalbo* (Western whores), UN madams, and Mrs. UN. The red-light district was called *Kijichon* (Military or Camp Town).

The report states that the reasons for establishing the brothels were:

1. To protect ordinary Korean women
2. To demonstrate the Korean government's appreciation to US troops
3. To raise soldiers' morale

Korean soldiers, as well as UN (US) soldiers, had access to comfort women.

As soon as the Korean Army's report concerning comfort women was published in 2002, the reference materials concerning comfort women who serviced Korean Army soldiers (located in the Reference Library of the Korean Ministry of National Defense) were declared off-limits. Kase-san concluded by saying, "I wonder if we can expect to see demonstrators erect statues of comfort women—this time in front of the Korean Parliament and the US Embassy."

Hiromichi Moteki and his essays are, recently, becoming well known among Tokyo correspondents. His essays are always logical and persuasive. Unfortunately, there seems to be no one else who consistently disseminates such rebuttals in English. Moteki's essays are known because they are meticulous and logically well-structured. I paid special attention to one of them, "The Truth about the Comfort Women," which appeared in the January 2012 issue of *Rekishi tsu* (*History Enthusiast*), published by WAC Magazines Co., Ltd.

Moteki skillfully uses Korean statements to support Japanese arguments. For example, he cites the remarks of Korean men attached to the Japanese Army found in a report entitled "Special Questions on Koreans," which is housed in the US National Archives. The men said, "All Korean prostitutes working in the Pacific Theater applied for such work of their own free will, or were sold by their parents. If the women had truly been abducted, Koreans, young and old, would have gone on a rampage and, heedless of possible repercussions, killed the Japanese."

Moteki comments: "This made perfect sense to me, as I know how proud the Korean people are. If women had been abducted, there would have been riots." He also points out the significance of something *not* said. "Strongman" Syngman Rhee was the Korean president who "implemented uncompromising anti-Japanese policies, making demand after demand, including reparations for having impressed Koreans into forced labor." Even he, however, "did not insist that reparations be paid to the comfort women, because such a demand would exceed the bounds of common sense. Rhee certainly knew that the comfort women were military prostitutes: everyone knew." That's how Moteki concludes his essay.[5]

OFFICIAL US DOCUMENT REVEALS THE TRUTH ABOUT COMFORT WOMEN

The very expression "comfort women" makes me uncomfortable, because the expression itself is a euphemism and I cannot accept it in a straightforward manner. It may be easier for the Japanese and Koreans to accept such a euphemistic expression, but for us foreign journalists, it sounds like an attempt to hide the truth or reality. I have to admit, however, that we too resort to euphemisms. Immediately after General MacArthur arrived at Atsugi, he ordered the establishment of brothels. Those patronized by American soldiers were named "recreation centers."

The expression "sex slave" is better understood, because it describes reality. Sex slaves were historical reality. For example, black slave women in America were treated as sex objects by their owners. Since we know about slavery and sex slaves, we feel and understand the reality. Gang rapes and massacres did take place, so we can understand them directly. "Sex slaves" is a horrible expression, but it is not alien, because they existed in fact.

"Comfort women," however, sounds like a horrible truth is being covered up, as though comfort women were something positive. The moment I heard the expression, I felt that it was hiding reality.

Slavery has never existed in Japan, nor is there any tradition of turning women into sex slaves. Japanese soldiers have never stooped to commit massacres or to rape women, unlike their counterparts from other countries. In other words, the Japanese have never resorted to tactics such as murder, robbery, rape, and so on, normally seen in the West. Japanese military personnel never resorted to robbery, rape and murder on the grand scale seen in other parts of the world. Japan does not have a culture that sets out to abduct women and make them into sex slaves. That is not how the country works.

During the Warring States era in Japan, battles were fought only among professional warriors and did not involve ordinary people. Peasants were spectators. When there was a battle, farmers went up the hill to watch it during lunch. After the Warring States era came the Edo era. The Tokugawa Shogunate was established, and peace prevailed for over 260 years until the Meiji Restoration.

We are not going into detail here on Edo culture. That is an entire subject in itself, but what we can say is that following the Meiji Restoration of 1867, there was no change in the fundamental Japanese mindset. This was still a place in which rape, robbery and massacre were considered to be the worst possible things that could happen.

The massacre of men and women, as well as gang rapes, were traditional in the Christian world. The best source of original insight into the topic of violence is probably the Old Testament. That part of the Bible is filled with exhortations to commit severe violence. In the Book of Numbers (31:17, 18) Moses addresses the people of Israel. He tells them to kill all Midianite males, including children, if they are to be delivered from their current predicament. He further orders the execution of all Midianite women who are not virgins. Virgins are to be distributed among the Israeli elite. This is pretty heavy stuff, coming as it does from the primary source of literature in our society.

But let us proceed to modern times. It is a fact that the defining event of WWII in Europe, in 1945, was the Soviet entry into Germany. What did Soviet troops do? They headed for Berlin, and along the way and in Berlin itself they indulged in the most extraordinary excesses, particularly sexual excesses. That was one occasion when sexual violence was witnessed in modern times in Europe. Soviet soldiers raped something like 100,000 German women, we are told.[6] Probably the number is much larger, but there you are.

Moving a little closer to modern times, still with that Hobbesian saying in mind ("life is nasty, brutish and short"), let us turn to Vietnam, the source of all the really bad things in society.

What did South Korean soldiers who were posted to Vietnam from their own country do in Vietnam? They cut loose and, like the Russian soldiers advancing on Berlin, they raped left, right and center. They murdered men and women; they treated men and women as objects.sIt was a very tough situation for all concerned. And just as tough were the consequences. When the tide of war receded in Vietnam, there were something like 30,000 babies of mixed Korean and Vietnamese blood, left behind on the beach.[7]

Well, the Americans did something about that. They introduced their Amerasian Immigration Act of 1982, which made provision for those mixed-race babies left behind on the battlefield. Thus it is that today we have still in Vietnam and in the United States, tens of thousands of these mixed-race babies, altogether several hundred thousand, we are told.

Now we move onward to the mid-twentieth century. Let us consider Japan and Southeast Asia. In Bandung, for example, later known as Indonesia (after having been called the Dutch East Indies for hundreds of years) some 80,000 Allied officers and men from the UK and the Netherlands, all commanded out of centers in Bandung, hid themselves in their fort in the middle of the city. They were attacked by a force of 800 Japanese soldiers. After only nine days of sporadic fighting, they surrendered. In Malaya, in the case of the British Army, and in Corregidor, in the case of the US Army, the Allied side actually surrendered after fighting for two months.

There were something like three million Japanese Army officers and soldiers located in the battlefields of Asia, from the north, all the way up to Manchuria through China, through Southeast Asia, and into the South Pacific Islands. These three million men committed no rapes. They were overseas for more than four years, coming and going. There are no records, however, of mixed-race babies. Not in the case of the Japanese. There was a sharp contrast there with the Korean Army, which left behind 30,000 mixed-race babies in Vietnam alone. Those babies, by the way, are known to Koreans as *Lai Dai Han*.

The comfort women system was introduced to avoid the occurrence of any sexual violence to innocent women in battle zones. The reality of Japanese comfort women who serviced Japanese military personnel is different from that of sex slaves.

One of the very earliest studies of comfort women is a report published in August 1944 by the United States Office of War Information Psychological Warfare Team. According to the report, the comfort woman was "nothing more than a prostitute." The women were "camp followers." I refer readers who are curious about camp followers to a scene in the movie *East of Eden* in which a prostitutes' wagon, a truckload full of these women, drives through a frontier where no women are to be found. Likewise, all over Asia, you had prostitutes trailing after the Japanese Army.

The same US report says that these prostitutes enjoyed picnics, sports, and dinner entertainment with Japanese officers and soldiers in their free time, and that these same women "were allowed to go back to their homes in Korea whenever they wanted." In addition they were allowed to refuse customers who were drunk.

"Slaves" is not the right word to use to describe the comfort women, because they were financially compensated for their services. While a Japanese soldier's monthly wage was ¥10, the comfort women, on average, were getting paid 30 times more than that monthly wage, or ¥300 per month.[8] They were certainly highly-paid prostitutes.

A Korean woman named Mun Ok-ju filed a case at the Tokyo District Court in the 1990s. She wished to withdraw savings she had accumulated working as a comfort woman from a Japanese bank. On investigation, her bank passbook was located. She had saved a huge amount (¥26,000) which, at that time, would have been enough to buy five houses in Tokyo just after the war.

Another case reported in the *Asahi Shimbun* involved a woman named Kim Hak-sun. The newspaper article quoted her as saying that she was forced to become a sex slave. She filed her case at the Tokyo District Court. In her legal statement, however, she said that her parents had sold her for ¥40 to a brothel run by a Korean. In other words, she was not abducted and forced into sex slavery. She herself admitted that she was merely a camp follower.[9]

The overall situation is described in Japanese War Ministry Document No. 2197, which states that anyone who resorts to recruiting methods that fraudulently employ the Army's name or that can be classified as abduction will be severely punished. Document No. 136 of the Interior Ministry Document No. 136 bans forced prostitution. Thus, there were no sex slaves associated with the Japanese Army.

A Korean newspaper reported that the Korean police arrested illegal operators and punished them. All through WWII, there was only one case of a Japanese soldier forcing Dutch women to work as prostitutes, in Semarang, Indonesia. The Japanese Army arrested the soldier who violated the prohibition against rape. After the war, Dutch authorities took over the military court, and all Japanese soldiers involved were executed.

The so-called sex-slaves were, in reality, camp followers chasing after the Japanese army. The accusation denigrates the Japanese military and the Japanese people. The Koreans proclaim that 200,000 Koreans were abducted and coerced to work as sex slaves. That sounds extremely dubious. The "sex slaves" were simply camp followers. According to Chiba University Professor Ikuhiko Hata, they were approximately 20,000 in number, and most of them (40%) were Japanese![10]

Kim Hak-Sun and other Korean comfort women were caught up in the Battle of Yue Teng, which took place in the western part of China, in the province of Yunnan, near the border with Myanmar. In September 1944 some 50,000 Chinese soldiers under the command of the US Army attacked a Japanese stronghold occupied by 1,200 troops. The Japanese fought for four months, but eventually faced the prospect of honorable death in battle (suicide). Just before the Japanese were defeated, their commander told the comfort women to surrender.

In the past, in China, many Japanese women had been raped and savagely killed by the Chinese in racist revenge. The fifteen Japanese comfort women, respecting the Japanese way of dying with honor, remained in the stronghold; all of them perished. The commander told the remaining five Korean women,

"You will not be killed because you are not Japanese." Those women walked down the hill and were captured by the US Army.

HOW TO RESOLVE THE COMFORT WOMEN CONTROVERSY

It was the Japanese who started using the expression "sex slaves." It attracted the attention of the foreign media and spread worldwide. No one else but the Japanese, who were at the epicenter, disseminated fabricated information about a massacre in Nanking or military prostitutes.

As reportage on the comfort women controversy became more extensive, the image of the Japanese as an evil race began to take hold throughout the world. The evil Japanese, and only the evil Japanese, abducted young women from anywhere and everywhere, and sold them to other parts of the world. The chief Cabinet secretary, Yohei Kono, created a great stink.[11] I don't know what we are going to say about Kono that hasn't been said already, but it was clear that the problem has not been resolved.

In Japan, it is possible to write off mistakes by apologizing. "Since an apology has been given, let's forgive the person" is a beautiful protocol for resolving conflicts among the Japanese people. Alas, in international society, apologizing means you are admitting that you have committed a sin, which must be compensated for accordingly.

What should Japan do, then? I think Japan should be absolutely open: clarify every fact and disseminate the truth. The comfort women controversy has been raging since 1996 and will continue to do so. I think it's obvious that propagandists in China and Korea have been utilizing it.

When I first visited Korea, I was a young foreign correspondent in my late 20s, so my curiosity about the people was considerable. At that age, you're not as easily seduced or dragged into other worlds as a younger person might be. I received no solicitations from prostitutes. Nor did I have any contact with them, except in one case. A Korean journalist friend encouraged me to go out one evening. He said he would take me someplace very exciting. This man, who was a good friend of mine, brought me to a little village full of houses, with maybe one or two women in each house, a real red-light district. I'd never seen one before. In any case, we arrived there and he went into one cabin. I went into another. After about five or seven minutes, I heard him shout. He said, maybe in Korean, or in English, "We're getting out of here. I'm going. Come, we're finished here." So I was a bit disappointed, but I accepted this. It wasn't my choice really, in the first place, but my friend wanted to have a bit of fun. For a 21-year old boy, it might be an amusing subject. But for a 29- or 30-year-old, it wasn't so much fun—not so interesting.

But I do remember going to Korea and staying in the Chosen Hotel in the late '70s. I took my wife there twice. The first time we stayed at the hotel, the front desk called us up and said, "You're occupying a room with someone of another nationality. Will you please come down and explain yourself?" I said, "There's no way I'm coming down." I didn't say I was with my wife, which I was.

Comfort women were not sex slaves. Prostitution was legal at the time of WWII. It is by and large the reality that prostitutes were hired by brothel operators and sold their services to soldiers. Among them, of course, were unfortunate women whose parents had sold them, due to poverty or something like that. Some of the young girls may not have even realized or been informed that they were sold by their parents. Sad as those cases were, they were commercial transactions. Soldiers snatching up young girls and carrying them away and forcing them into sexual slavery is another story. Japan had nothing to do with that. Japan did not do that.

The question then becomes, "How did this accusation arise?" I think it's in part Korean propaganda, but mostly it's Japanese propaganda. Japanese are accusing other Japanese. The expression "sex slaves" was first used not by the Koreans, but by the Japanese themselves.

Another point is the notion that such sexual activities did not take place at all. This is kind of far-fetched. Friends of Japan are skeptical when we're told there were no rapes, none at all. Such a position flies in the face of common sense. If it's true—and I don't want to deny that this is totally untrue—then rapes would never be committed in this country. It would have been remarkable if no rapes were committed by Japanese officers or soldiers, but Akira Kurosawa certainly did not believe that.

Kurosawa's famous movie, *Rashomon*, is essentially a story revolving around a question. The question is, "Was a rape committed?" Kurosawa provides no answer. He doesn't tell us what happened. He presents five different interpretations of the events that took place. It's a very complex, highly regarded movie. Foreigners who love Japan, myself included, worry about extreme views like "there were no rapes at all."

NOTES

1. The transcript of the press conference can be found at http://ajw.asahi.com/article/behind_news/politics/AJ201305270012.

2. Bungei Shunju, the best-known general monthly magazine in Japan.

3. Supreme Commander for Allied Powers.

4. http://www.sdh-fact.com/CL/Women2e.pdf

5. http://www.sdh-fact.com/essay-article/320.

6. *Berlin the Downfall 1945*, by Anthony Beevor, New York, NY: Viking, 2002.

7. Coleman, Norm. "President Park Should Publicly Apologize for South Korea's Sexual Violence in Vietnam | Fox News." *Fox News.* FOX News Network, 13 Oct. 2015. Web. 19 Jan. 2016.

8. http://www.sdh-fact.com/CL02_1/84_S4.pdf. Also see http://www.sdh-fact.com/CL02_4/8_S1.pdf, in which the average earing is recorded ¥750 per month.

9. Discussed in http://www.sdh-fact.com/CL02_1/84_S4.pdf.

10. Hata, Ikuhiko. *Ianfu to Senjo No Sei*. Tokyo: Shinchosha, 1999. Print.

11. The Kono Statement, issued in 1993, acknowledges that the Japanese Army coerced women, either directly or indirectly, into serving as military prostitutes.

Chapter Five

Chiang Kai-shek and Mao Zedong Silent about "Nanking Massacre"

The so-called Nanking Massacre was a propaganda strategy launched in China in the context of an intelligence war waged in 1937–38. As such, the "Nanking Massacre" was a flat-out winner, an odds-on, solid-gold hit, and a screaming success, for to this day not a soul has objected to the accusation. Thus far, the cost has been minimal, and the impact maximal! What the KMT intelligence tacticians did was hire an Australian hack called Harold Timperley in early 1938. Timperley was China correspondent for the *Manchester Guardian*; he was based in Shanghai. He was hired to write a book based on copy supplied by his KMT colleagues. The resulting volume, published in London later that year, was entitled *What War Means*. The KMT's strategy worked far better than anyone—China's intelligence bosses under Chiang Kai-shek included—had expected. It is still working. Thank you very much! The book persuaded everyone that a Guernica-like event transpired in Nanking in December 1937, when the forces of the Mikado ran amok for weeks and devastated the city, the most ancient imperial capital of China. The point is clear. The Japanese—no one else—had to be the villains of this story.

Every now and then the Foreign Correspondents' Club of Japan (FCCJ) invites the author of a popular book to give a lecture. The event is called Book Break. We invited Professor Minoru Kitamura of Ritsumeikan University to speak about what is called the Nanking Incident in Japan. Minoru Kitamura[1] graduated from Kyoto University in 1973, studied at the graduate school of the same university for four years and then taught at Mie University. Kitamura subsequently became a professor at Ritsumeikan University in Kyoto, where he taught modern Chinese history.

Professor Kitamura wrote *The Politics of Nanjing* (originally published by *Bunshun Shinsho* in 2001, and issued in English by the *University Press of*

49

America, Inc. in 2007). Traveling with his interpreter all the way from Kyoto to Tokyo, he paid all costs out of his own pocket (the FCCJ does not cover speakers' expenses). Journalists are always suspicious. What it takes to be a journalist is the ability to doubt. We do not have any other talents. We do not believe till we see the facts. That is how we are trained.

Having heard Professor Kitamura's lecture for the first time, I was awakened to the facts regarding the "Nanking Massacre." Until then, I simply trusted the "thesis" proclaimed in America and Europe: the Japanese Army committed a massacre in Nanking in 1937. After Professor Kitamura's Book Break, I made time to do some research myself to learn about what really happened in Nanking. Many Japanese—reporters from major news organizations, professors, even Foreign Ministry officials and diplomats – believe the "Nanking Massacre" actually took place. I learned, however, that this was Allied propaganda. This is, in a way, my anti-thesis of the "Nanking Massacre."

I am neither a historian nor an authority on the Nanking issue. However, I am confident that the "Nanking Massacre" was propaganda initiated by the Chinese CIA in the intelligence war. The Chinese intelligence organization had a very close relationship with H.J. Timperley, China correspondent for the *Manchester Guardian*.

Timperley wrote a book entitled, *What War Means: The Japanese Terror in China*, which was published in London and New York. The collection of his writings on the criminal brutalities of the Japanese Army during its occupation of Nanking was published very soon after the occupation, and shocked Western intellectual society. It was accepted as objective reportage written by a journalist who had witnessed horrific scenes with his own eyes. However, it has now become clear that Timperley was deeply involved with the intelligence arm of the KMT government's Central Propaganda Department.

Timperley's *What War Means* has a red hard cover on which the words "Left Book Club" are printed, along with "not for sale to the public." The publisher was Victor Gollancz, Ltd., of London. According to Kitamura's research, the Left Book Club was founded in 1936 as an organization of left-wing intellectuals; the Communist Party of Great Britain and the Comintern supported the publishing activities of the Left Book Club.

Timperley was also introduced in the *Biographical Dictionary of Foreigners in China in the Modern Age*, published by the Chinese Social Sciences Publishing Co. as follows: "After the Marco Polo Bridge Incident, the KMT dispatched him to Europe and the United States to engage in propaganda activities. Following this, he was employed as advisor to the KMT's Chinese Ministry of Information."

In *Research on KMT's News Administration Policy, 1928–45* published in Taiwan by the KMT Central Party Committee Publishers in 1996, there is a section concerning the Nanking Incident:

When the world was shaken by the Japanese Army's evil actions in the Great Massacre at Nanking, the China Information Committee immediately hired the *Manchester Guardian* journalist, Timperley, and the American professor, Smythe, who were both in Nanking at that time, to produce propaganda materials for us, titled *Facts of the Japanese Army's Violence* and *A True Description of War Damages in Nanking*. Both these books immediately became famous. In this way, the Chinese themselves did not come to the forefront, but by paying money and through other means, an international friend who understands the truth and methods of our war of resistance became a spokesman for us in a roundabout propaganda manner, which was one of the most commonly used techniques of the China Information Committee during the war. The results were remarkable.

Professor Kitamura singles out Zeng Xubai, the chief of the China Information Committee, who comments on his relationship with Timperley in his *Autobiography*:

Timperley was very convenient when we were developing our anti-Japanese international propaganda in Shanghai. He was one of three important people who joined the War Resistance Committee. (. . .) We contacted him as soon as he arrived in Shanghai from Nanking. We then flew him from Hong Kong to Hankow to meet with us and we discussed everything directly. . . . At that stage, it would be absolutely no good for us Chinese to show our faces, and we decided that we would have to search for international friends who understand the facts of our war of resistance and our policy, and for such people to be our spokespersons. Timperley was an ideal choice. Thus, we decided that our first step would be to make payment to Timperley, and also, through his coordination, to Smythe, and commission both of them to write and publish two books for us as witnesses to the Nanking Massacre. [2]

Likewise, some of the most important documents with information about the "Nanking Massacre" broadcast to the world at the time were manipulated by the Chinese CIA. Their propaganda activities constituted a large-scale operation, as explained by Zeng Xubai:

We held discussions with Timperley and he became our secret man in charge of propaganda in America for the China Information Committee. Timperley and we agreed that he would handle the flow of news under the name Trans-Pacific News Service. At the same time, we decided that Earl Leaf be assigned to the New York office, Henry Evans to the Chicago office and Malcom Rosholt to the San Francisco office. These were all experienced American journalists. [3]

Most of Zeng Xubai's propaganda bases were in America, but he also established one in London, ostensibly a branch office of the Trans-Pacific News Service. So, from scratch, the "Nanking Massacre" was propaganda created by the KMT government, and Timperley acted as an intelligence agent for

the KMT. Professor Kitamura makes two points in *The Politics of Nanjing*:
(1) various Western journalists were involved with the Chinese CIA, and (2)
China's propaganda organization was confident, through their activities, that
Westerners were worth fully utilizing.

It is obvious that Timperley was paid by the Chinese CIA, but how much
he was paid is unknown. Kitamura mentioned in his book that it was Timperley who proclaimed to the world that 300,000 civilians were massacred in
Nanking. Where on earth did this number come from? At the beginning of
1938, China's intelligence agency was not yet well-organized. Timperley's
magnificent result must have surprised the Chinese CIA. Their propaganda
was a great success. The Chinese had the world believing that the Japanese
were barbarians and the Chinese were angels.

WESTERNERS ENCIRCLED
BY THE KMT'S CENTRAL PROPAGANDA DEPARTMENT

Professor Shudo Higashinakano of Asia University is a well-known authority
on the Nanking Incident. A book he published, *Top-Secret Chinese Nationalist Documents Reveal the Truth About the Nanking Incident*[4] contains a lot of
surprising facts.

*Overview of Propaganda Operations of the International Propaganda
Division of the Central Propaganda Bureau*, a formerly top-secret document,
states:

> The best result would be gained by getting foreign journalists to publish our
> propaganda texts unchanged; but if the propaganda texts we put out are to be
> published by foreign journalists, we first have to gain their confidence. These
> operations are truly troublesome and difficult, but we absolutely have to do
> them carefully.[5]

The IPD (International Propaganda Division), which organized resident
foreign correspondents of all newspapers, and foreign military officials and
news specialists in China, held 300 press conferences in the 11 months from
December 1, 1937 to October 4, 1938. However, the IPD did not use the
word *massacre*, not even once.

According to *Overview of Propaganda Operations*, foreign correspondents cooperated with the IPD in rigorous and thorough screening:

> After every telegram had received an introductory-level screening and if there
> was no problem, the censor applied the Division's "Passed Screening" stamp
> and it was then sent to the telegraph office for transmission. If there was any
> censoring, it was stamped either "Passed With ____ Characters Censored" or
> "Entire Text Censored."[6]

Whether actively or after the fact, foreign correspondents had to go through this screening by the IPD.

On November 17, 1937, the International Committee was formed to create a safety zone for the protection of noncombatants. On November 22 John Rabe was selected to be the International Committee's spokesman. He was the Nanking branch manager of the German firm Siemens AG. The IPD's approach to the International Committee was thorough as well. At about this time, the CPB (Central Propaganda Bureau) started holding tea parties and press conferences in Nanking. On November 23, Rabe wrote in his journal:

> 5 p.m.: Tea party given by Mr. Zhang Qun, former foreign minister and now chief secretary of the Ministry of Foreign Affairs. In addition to about 50 Americans and Europeans from various countries, the party was attended by: General Tang, who is in charge of the defense of the city; General Wang Gupan, the chief of police, and Ms. Chaojun, the mayor. The "main idea" is that the remaining Europeans and Americans are all to gather each evening between eight and nine o'clock at the International Club, so that we can maintain contact with leading Chinese figures or their representatives. [7]

The International Club, managed by the KMT, was established to facilitate exchanges between Chinese residents and foreigners. From 8:30 to 9:30, people from embassies, business, churches and the press met representatives from the Army, the police and the city. Making use of such a privilege and screening, the IPD began to encircle them. The effect was surprising. When foreign journalists submitted various questions about the government, economy, transportation, money market, industry, or the social situation, they asked for the views of the responsible authorities. In this manner, the IPD paid scrupulous attention in dealing with them even though it was truly troublesome and difficult. It goes without saying that they had journalists write articles for them in accordance with the expectations of the CPB. For that purpose, the CBP's International Propaganda Division was paying extremely careful attention:

> Foreign journalists have a considerably frank sentiment, so this Division deals with them in a sincere manner. Most of them deeply sympathize with our country, but journalists by temperament will always write down what they hear, and they are quite capable of picking up rumors and sending off telegrams to report what they have heard. As an expression rife with implications, they excel at cleverly escaping the censors' attention. If the telegrams dispatched by foreign journalists living in China are published in newspapers all over the world, people overseas who are observing the situation in the Far East would consider them with importance, so it is necessary to make a thorough and rigorous screening of these reports. Those telegrams lacking in propriety were either censored or prohibited, and then the reason was explained to the

sender and we attempted to gain reliable consent to amend the mistaken view-points. [8]

They say that China has a 4,000-year-old history. However it is completely different from that of Japan, which has been under one dynasty, under one imperial family line. In China, whenever a mandate to rule the country was given to a new dynasty, previous histories were rejected, and new ones written. China also has a 4,000-year history of fabricating historical facts. That is the essence of Chinese history. The "Nanking Massacre" is a good example of the use of a refined technique to create history.

JOURNALISTS WHO "COVERED" THE "NANKING MASSACRE"

There were two foreign journalists who issued reports on the "Nanking Massacre." They were Frank Tillman Durdin of *The New York Times* and Archibald Steele of the *Chicago Daily News*. On December 15, the third day of the Japanese occupation of Nanking, there being no electricity in that city, they headed off to Shanghai to transmit their articles about the Japanese Army's battle in Nanking.

On the 15th, Steele sent out the first report on the occupation of Nanking; it appeared the next day (but was dated the 15th in America owing to the International Date Line) as the lead story in the *Chicago Daily News* under the headline "Account of Massacre in Nanking."

> "Four days in hell" would be the most fitting way to describe the siege and capture of Nanking. (. . .) The story of Nanking's fall is a story of indescribable panic and confusion among the entrapped Chinese defenders, followed by a reign of terror by the conquering army which cost thousands of lives, many of them innocent ones. (. . .) It was like killing sheep. (. . .) This account is based on the observations of myself and other foreigners remaining in Nanking throughout the siege.

Durdin's article was carried in *The New York Times* on December 18.

> Wholesale looting, the violation of women, the murder of civilians . . . turned Nanking into a city of terror. (. . .) Any person who ran because of fear or excitement was likely to be killed on the spot. (. . .) Many slayings were witnessed by foreigners.

Expressions like "many of them innocent ones" and "murder of civilians" give the impression that civilians were slaughtered. Such killings would have been serious violations of international law. The mass killing of civilians could only have been a massacre.

As I have previously explained, Timperley, the *Manchester Guardian's* China correspondent issued a book entitled *What War Means* in July 1938. This is the book which compiled letters and memoranda of an anonymous American who witnessed the entire event, before and after the Fall of Nanking. In fact, the book earned a huge reputation after the identities of the anonymous writers were revealed. They were Miner Searle Bates, a member of the International Committee and a professor at the University of Nanking, and George Fitch, another member of the International Committee and a Christian missionary. Bates attended the Tokyo Trials to testify of the atrocities committed by the Japanese Army.

Zeng Xubai, the chief of the China Information Committee, wrote in his autobiography that the Central Propaganda Bureau made payments to Timperley, commissioned him to write a book, and succeeded in having it published. Bates and Fitch were not independent third-party observers at all.[9]

Bates was an adviser to the Chinese central government. Fitch's wife was a close personal friend of Soong Chingling, the wife of Chiang Kai-shek. Bates said that the book, referring to *What War Means*, included a report he handed to journalists leaving Nanking on December 15, asking them to make use of it. Among the journalists were Steele and Durdin. The "report" stated:

> "But in two days the whole outlook has been ruined by frequent murder, wholesale and semi regular looting, and uncontrolled disturbance of private homes including offences against the security of women. Foreigners who have traveled over the city report many civilian bodies lying in the streets (. . .) A considerable percentage of the dead civilians were the victims of shooting or bayoneting in the afternoon and evening of the 13th, which was the time of the Japanese entry into the city. (. . .) Squads of men picked out by Japanese troops as former Chinese soldiers have been tied together and shot. These soldiers had discarded their arms, and in some cases their military clothing (. . .) Surely this horrible exhibition in Nanking does not represent the best achievement of the Japanese Empire . . . ."[10]

NOT A SINGLE WITNESS TO MURDER

However, the above-mentioned "report" does not reflect descriptions in the reports of serious injuries to civilians, the most fundamental historical records, which were sent to the Japanese Embassy by foreigners in Nanking who comprised the International Committee. These reports of serious injuries to civilians were compiled into a single set by the hand of Prof. Lewis Smythe in February 1938. One hundred twenty-three cases out of a total of 444 were included as an appendix to *What War Means*. After that, they were published in the summer of 1939 in English as *Documents of the Nanking Safety Zone*,[11] under the editorial supervision of the Council of International Affairs, which was directed by Chiang Kai-shek's Military Affairs Commission. Let us look at all the incidents reported for three days from December 13 to 15.

> Dec. 13: Murders, zero incidents; rapes, four incidents; looting, three incidents; arson, zero incidents; kidnapping, one incident; injuries, one incident; trespass, zero incidents.
> Dec. 14: Murders, one incident; rapes, four incidents; looting, three incidents; arson, zero incidents; kidnapping, one incident; injuries, zero incidents; trespass, one incident.
> Dec. 15: Murders, four incidents; rapes, five incidents; looting, five incidents; arson, zero incidents; kidnapping, one incident; injuries, five incidents; trespass, two incidents.

These are not statistics prepared by the Japanese. They are a record of incident reports the International Committee received from residents of Nanking, which was then submitted to the Japanese Embassy. There are no witnessed murders. It should be clear that there is no basis for truth in Steele and Durdin's assertions that "many slayings were witnessed by foreigners."

Bates must have compiled a false report based on the Central Propaganda Bureau's plan to expose "outrages committed by the enemy." Neither Steele nor Durdin may have ever imagined that Bates, a trusted missionary, would tell a lie. Neither Steele nor Durdin checked the validity of a report compiled by a man they trusted. But Bates certainly did lie.

Steele and Durdin won the historical honor of becoming the first two foreign correspondents who reported the "Nanking Massacre" to the world. Steele and Durdin, however, did not testify to "frequent civilian murders" at the Tokyo Trials. The "Nanking Massacre" articles written by Steele and Durdin were based on reports of events that transpired over three days, which were submitted by people who were actually there. Later Nanking articles described how the indiscriminate killing of civilians was spreading. China's representative to the League of Nations, Gu Weijin, addressed the League on February 2, 1938, stating that 20,000 people had been killed (his address was based on the aforementioned newspaper articles).

If his claim had been accurate, the governments of every nation would immediately have moved to control the situation. It seems, however, that nothing was done; the claim was simply ignored.

CRITICAL EVIDENCE OF THE FABRICATION OF THE "NANKING MASSACRE"

In April 1938, four months after Nanking fell, Cabot Coville, the military attaché at the American Embassy in Tokyo, arrived in Nanking to conduct an investigation. Consul John Allison and others, Bates included, met with Coville to apprise him of the situation in Nanking.

Coville stated in his report that "looting and rapes by the Japanese soldiers continued for some weeks, and when Allison arrived at 11 a.m. on January 6 to reopen the Embassy, it was still going on." What should be noted is that his report made no mention of killings or massacres. In spite of the fact that Bates was there, his report never touches upon a single civilian murder.

When coverage of the "Nanking Massacre" appeared in American newspapers, the KMT government should have expressed outrage and complained about the Japanese. In truth, however, Gu Weijin, a prominent figure in Chinese diplomatic circles, made only brief mention of the situation in Nanking in his address to the League of Nations based on American news reports, but these massacre stories had no appeal at all at the 100th Assembly of the League of Nations.

In fact, more surprising than Coville's making no mention of killings or a "massacre" is the fact that the KMT government never used the expression "Nanking Massacre" as a propaganda tool to appeal to international society, in spite of the fact that American news reported on the "Japanese Army's massacre." Four months after the Fall of Nanking, the inaugural issue of the monthly magazine *China at War* appeared. It contained no reference in to a "Nanking Massacre" as reported by Durdin and Steele. The truth is, if one reads the inaugural issue of *China at War,* which followed a policy of describing only the facts, based on official announcements, one finds that all it had to say about Nanking is this: "Nanking—after December 12, 1937— became a hunting ground for the Japanese soldiers who combed the city looking for money, loot and women." The word *massacre* never appeared.

If the American newspaper articles had been accurate, would not the KMT government, the CPB, and the Republic of China's Foreign Service have boldly repeated them over and over in public forums, complaining about the "Nanking Massacre" to the whole world? Using the diplomatic route, surely they would have repeatedly protested to the Japanese government. In point of fact, there is not one such instance.

Moreover, both Bates and Fitch were in the Safety Zone in the City of Nanking. As previously explained, there were few reported "murder" cases, let alone massacres. On top of that, among those few cases, there were zero cases of a murder that was actually witnessed. Bates and Fitch recorded the "murder of 12,000 civilian men and women in three days" and the "murder of 30,000 soldiers." Where on earth did such murders take place?

Steele wrote in his article in the *Chicago Daily News* that during the three days between December 12 and 15, "there was a band of 300 Chinese being methodically executed before the wall near the waterfront." He reported the "execution of Chinese soldiers" as "the execution of Chinese." The world knew of the Japanese Army's executions after mopping-up operations were complete, but no country made any complaints to Japan based on this incident. It is all the more notable that the KMT government, far from criticizing Japan, ignored the situation.

Chinese soldiers removed by the Japanese Army from the Safety Zone were registered as civilians unless they were being a nuisance. Defeated soldiers were put to work as coolies, and treated well. A Japanese Army private's base pay per month was five and a half yen. In comparison, a coolie was paid five yen a month.

What War Means is the book Timperley wrote on the request of the Central Propaganda Bureau. The book was translated into a Chinese-language version called *Japanese Military Atrocities Witnessed by Foreigners*. The two anonymous "foreign residents of Nanking" have been identified as Miner Searle Bates and George Fitch. In Bates' personal history, in the Yale University archives, he recorded that, "In Timperley's volume, Chapter I & II came from George Fitch; except pp. 18–20 from me, also III, IVa and Appendix F."

The CPB, however, conducted editorial operations that can only be called strange and contradictory. They removed lines (1) and (2), which were in Chapter III of the English version of *What War Means*, when they produced the Chinese version:

> Sentence (1): Burial gangs report three thousand bodies at that point, left in rows or piles after mass execution.
> Sentence (2): Evidence from burials indicates that close to forty thousand unarmed persons were killed within and near the walls of Nanking, of whom some 30 per cent had never been soldiers.

The Central Propaganda Bureau took it for granted that readers of the English-language version of *What War Means* were foreigners living overseas and therefore could not tell whether the descriptions in it were true or not. The Chinese-language version, however, would be read by people living on the Chinese mainland. They would have had good knowledge of the situation, and upon seeing Sentences (1) and (2) in *What War Means*, would know they weren't true, and would condemn the book as mere propaganda. So the CPB deleted both sentences from the Chinese version.

It is understandable that the CPB deleted the sentenced describing the murder of 40,000 from the Chinese version. What is more astonishing, however, is the fact that Bates agreed to delete his claim of "the illegal murder of 40,000 civilians" from that version.

Here is an even more surprising fact: The Anti-Enemy Section of the CPB's International Propaganda Division summarized *What War Means* in a formerly top-secret document entitled "Summary of Anti-Enemy Section Operations" as follows:

> Japanese Atrocities Witnessed by Foreigners
>   This book was written by the famous English journalist Timperley. The book records detailed accounts of heinous acts—rape, arson, looting – and a breakdown in military discipline and circumstances of depraved human conditions after the enemy entered Nanking in Dec. 13, 1937. In addition to publishing this book in Chinese and in English, it was also translated into Japanese. The Japanese edition's title was changed to *What is War?* The preface of the Japanese edition is by Japanese antiwar writer Aoyama Kazuo, and there are many photographs of brutality inside. This book was widely sold in Hong Kong, Shanghai, and everywhere overseas as well. Afterward, the enemy's chief of the General Staff, Prince Kan'in, published a book to inform officers and men of the Japanese army, acknowledging that this was conduct disgraceful to the nation and the Imperial Army in China, and to admonish them. [12]

Surprisingly enough, this summary does not even mention the word *murder*, let alone *massacre* or *slaughter*. The only possible explanation for this is that the KMT government, the CPB, and the IPD knew there had been no massacre in Nanking. If the "Nanking Massacre" was a historical fact, they should have used the expression *massacre* for propaganda purposes in a massive way.

For the Japanese Army the Battle of Nanking was a military operation whose purpose was to attack the enemy's capital; it took place, in fact, under the world's scrutiny. Its chief commander, General Iwane Matsui, exercised strict ethical control over his officers and men, so that the Imperial Army would never do anything that would disgrace the honor of the Emperor.

Professor Higashinakano's research is thorough when it comes to the Nanking Incident and I would like to express my sincere respect for his devotion. His arguments are well explained and also backed up by detailed evidence he found to support his claims.

Additionally, I learned from Hideaki Kase that both Chiang Kai-shek and Mao Zedong made a lot of addresses after the Fall of Nanking, but they did not mention even once that the Japanese Army resorted to murder in Nanking. From this fact alone, we can understand that the "Nanking Massacre" is a fabrication.

WHAT I LEARNED FROM THE KWANGJU INCIDENT

Finally, I would like to say that it was extremely difficult to grasp objectively what was really happening at Nanking at that time. I can say this from my experience as a journalist.

In May of 1980, I was on the spot when the Kwangju[13] Uprising took place in South Korea. Kwangju is the capital of the southern province called South Jeolla, which is about three hours away from Seoul. Its population, according to 1970 statistics, is 502,753.

I was the Tokyo Bureau Chief of *The New York Times* back then and I entered Gwangju to report on what had happened. In the afternoon of the day I arrived there, I attempted to find out, first of all, how many people were killed, and where they were killed.

In Kwangju I found many foreign correspondents. What I learned there at that time was that in a city of that size it was extremely difficult to grasp what was happening during an armed confrontation. I saw dead bodies lying on the ground. I heard gunshots. But I was not able to tell who was shooting at whom, why the shooting started, who was taking the initiative on the civilians' side, what kind of person the leader of this incident was, or whether he knew what was going on.

My reports to *The New York Times* headquarters on that day and the following day were not sufficient in content at all. At the time of the incident, correspondents from other Western media companies were writing completely different reports from mine. We were all at the site of the incident, but the reports turned out to be different. Of course, journalists want to write reports that differ from others in nature and viewpoint, but the differences were too great in that case.

It was still not clear what had happened in Kwangju in May 1980, even after 10 years had passed. The truth came out after 20 years. I co-authored and published a book on Kwangju in English with a friend of mine, Jae Lee.[14] We compiled the reports of ten Western journalists, myself included, who were at site when the Kwangju Incident took place. From this experience, I learned that it is difficult to grasp what is going on even one block away.

Bradley Martin of the *Baltimore Sun* in America wrote excellent reports. His source was a student leader who initiated a battle against the army. I met him, in fact, on the afternoon of the day he died.

No matter what we reported, random murders were taking place and the victims were civilians. Not even one was wearing a military uniform. Some local police chiefs and officers engaged in combat like cruel gangsters. They were possibly Kim Dae-jung supporters, but we cannot tell even now.

In Nanking Bates was a source for Western journalists. He played the major role of reporting the "Nanking Massacre." He produced figures such as "the murder of 12,000 civilian men, women and children in 3 days" and "the murder of 30,000 soldiers." Ten years after the Fall of Nanking, Bates testified to that effect at the court of the Tokyo Trials. We contacted exactly the same kinds of people in Kwangju. We regard such people as important, since they can confirm exactly what is taking place. But in reality, we just couldn't accurately grasp what was going on at that time: how many people were killed, or the name of the student leader I just referred to, for example. I learned his name twenty years later.

I can clearly say that what happened in Nanking in 1937 was not grasped by the journalists who were on the spot at that time. People started evacuating from Nanking in the summer of 1937. This was natural, given that they had learned about the KMT's defeat in Shanghai.

According to the report of the International Committee, the number of people who remained in Nanking at the time of the battle was 200,000. But after the Fall of Nanking, the population started to increase, reaching 250,000 in the following month, January 1938. Combat ended and peace was restored, so people returned to Nanking.

From this it is clear that the "Nanking Massacre" did not take place. As a historical fact, the "Nanking Massacre" never existed. It was originally a propaganda tool fabricated by the KMT government.

NOTES

1. Prof. Kitamura Minoru , http://www.sdh-fact.com/CL02_1/78_S3.pdf.

2. Kitamura Minoru, The Politics of Nanjing: An Impartial Investigation, trans. Hal Gold (Lanham, Maryland: University Press of America, 2006), p. 30.

3. Ibid., p. 31.

4. Higashinakano Shudo, Top-Secret Chinese Nationalist Documents Reveal the Truth About the Nanking Incident , http://www.sdh-fact.com/CL02_1/27_S4.pdf.

5. Ibid., p. 33.

6. Ibid., p. 42.

7. Ibid., p. 53.

8. Ibid., p. 41.

9. Zeng Xubai, Zeng Xubai zizhuan (Autobiography of Zeng Xubai) (Taipei: Lianjing chuban shiye gongsi, 1988–90).

10. Higashinakano, op. cit., p. 96.

11. Shuhsi Hsü, ed. Documents of the Nanking Safety Zone, Prepared under the Auspices of the Council of International Affairs, Chungking (Shanghai, Kelly & Walsh Limited, 1939).

12. Higashinakano, op. cit., pp. 169–170.

13. Today more commonly known as Gwangju.

14. Henry Scott-Stokes and Jae-Eui Lee, eds. The Kwangju Uprising: Eyewitness Press Accounts of Korea's Tiananmen (Armonk: M.E. Sharpe, 2000).

Chapter Six

What Was the Meaning of
Voices of the Heroic Dead?

DIMENSIONAL DIFFERENCE OF THE EMPEROR SHOWA
AS THE HEAD OF STATE

I think the point to make about Mishima is that he did everything on a big scale. In other words, you might say he was incapable of being boring. Every topic he broached was magnified the second he opened his mouth. He was not only incapable of being boring, he was right out there by himself. There was nobody competing with him in terms of vividness of expression. He was a master of colorful remarks.

As to the specific topic of the Greater East Asian War, my impression is that his father had enormous influence on him. Azusa Hiraoka was a very cynical bureaucrat with a cynical attitude towards the war. He thought that Japan was going to lose, and that it would be best to make preparations for the time after the Greater East Asian War had come to an end. I think the Hiraoka family was being very realistic about the likely outcome of the war. One of the vital events for people in that frame of mind was the so-called Doolittle Raid of 1942. The bombing of Japan began in earnest two years after the Doolittle Raid due to two factors: Saipan was captured in 1944 by American forces and B-29s, which were made available in 1944, were based in Saipan and within striking distance from Japan. So when we look at Mishima's idealism, his nationalism, the pride he had in this country, all these really originated with his father.

What Mishima himself was interested in was that which would go on forever. He felt there was something about Japan that was completely unique, something that was totally unseen by foreigners, and something that would never be understood by foreigners: the Japanese essence. He was very proud of this country. He didn't think that the impending defeat was in itself of great importance.

So the ceremony on the *Missouri*, for example, never attracted him at all. He didn't get wrapped up in discussing Perry, either. He may have had views, but if so, he didn't express them. These were marginal topics. What he was interested in was the spiritual side of his country and cultural tradition. This was a long way from the position that others took. His originality appealed to the Gakushuin teachers who educated him, especially Shino-san. If one reads about Mishima when he was 15 years old, one will discover that he was ahead of everybody else, even at that time. And Shino himself was held in such high regard. He was the person who, on remembering viewing scenic Mr. Fuji from the little town of Mishima, thought that the name Mishima might suit the brilliant young man better than Hiraoka (Mishima's family name, his grandfather's name).

What was the Emperor to Mishima? Here we have to reckon with the fact that this emperor, Showa Tenno, was adored as a figure of worship. But again, realistically, some Japanese harbored the rather cynical view that Showa Tenno was not a brilliant man. This was brought home to me by a man called Ichiro Hattori of the Seiko Corporation's Hattori family. Ichiro-san is the one who created the Epson brand. He died very young, in his early fifties. He worked too hard.

I saw him in London two or three weeks before he died, from a heart attack. He started talking about the Emperor. He knew that I was interested, as I had done the Mishima book, and he was prepared to advance plenty of financial support for me to do research. He brought up the topic of Showa Tenno because he wanted me to understand his point of view. He said that in his opinion (and among people of his caliber in Tokyo) the sense was that this emperor had, roughly speaking, the intellect of a primary school teacher. His point was that if the Emperor had had a higher level of intelligence, he couldn't have been controlled by the Army, and thus the war could have been possibly avoided. Hattori studied at Yale. During his lifetime he was much more interested in golf and business than the history of Japan.

This is the kind of cynical view held by some people. It is an argument that looks at the Emperor from a down-to-earth perspective as mere human being. But the existence of the Emperor has a totally different value from that of national leaders, such as presidents or prime ministers, who are elected by the people. Emperor Showa was the leader of a country defeated in war. Nonetheless, he remained in his position as the Emperor of Japan and continued to enjoy the respect of the Japanese people, even immediately after the war. This was an unprecedented situation. It is a miracle for a national leader to remain in his position after a defeat in war. A national leader who loses a war is usually executed or exiled. An exiled leader will be a target of assassination.

Emperor Showa was in a different dimension in this respect. He traveled all over Japan immediately after the defeat, without tight security. Moreover, he was enthusiastically welcomed by the people everywhere he went. Asked about the Emperor by the press at the end of the Tokyo Trials, the chief jurist, Webb, said that the Emperor is a "god."

But differing views can coexist: the view that acknowledges the Emperor as a spiritual leader, a cultural symbol, and Hattori's perception of him as irrelevant. The role ordained by the Imperial Constitution, which the Emperor was forced to play, was a little too political. However, it doesn't detract from the symbolism, the importance of the Emperor himself. Everybody gathered around him. The photograph of the Emperor at Ichigaya surrounded by Army and Navy officers is a fantastic picture. There is no such picture out of Chinese history that I know of, or Korean. There is no such picture from the Anglo powers during the war, so we Westerners haven't got anything to compare with this in the UK or in the US. The symbolism is tremendously important. His appearance immediately after the Pearl Harbor attack on his white horse, that too was an incredible moment. So his actual level of intelligence was not so important, compared with his existence as a symbol.

Hattori undoubtedly thought that the Emperor should have been able to intervene earlier than he actually did, and should have served his country better in that sense. I sense that sort of attitude among historians in the West: if only he had had a little more force of character, the events of history might have been quite different. What I am trying to say is that Mishima knew all of this, and had moved past this sort of limited understanding to a much greater concept: this country is worthwhile. The Emperor is a divine existence in this country.

MISHIMA'S CRITICISM OF THE EMPEROR'S "DECLARATION OF HUMANITY"

There is a biography of Meiji Tenno by Donald Keene. It's a 900-page book. In the book, there are pages on the death of Emperor Komei, Meiji's father. Keene advances the theory that Emperor Komei was murdered, speculates on how the crime was committed, and names people who harbored the same suspicions at the time of Emperor Komei's death.

I asked Keene whether he had any trouble with the right wing as a result. He said two men visited him once briefly when he was doing his research, but they never came back again. This human side of the throne of the Imperial institution exists as a fact. Emperors are human beings, and they are separately divine beings of the kind that people greatly respect. The two aspects are not necessarily conflicting. They can exist at the same time, and they do.

MacArthur wanted to deny Tenno's divinity. That's why he had the Emperor issue what is known as the "Declaration of Humanity" on New Year's Day in 1946. This was meaningless, because even if a god declares, "I am not a god," his divinity will not be lost. Tenno did not make himself a god. Emperor Showa simply stated that he never attempted to use his divinity to conquer the world. He never denied his divinity in the declaration.

I don't think Yukio would have taken that declaration very seriously. I mean I don't think he would have been disturbed by it, because it was on such a low level. The point was made once in the Emperor's New Year's speech in 1946. Of course, Yukio profoundly objected to this characterization. He opposed the attitude that did not recognize the Emperor as *arahito-gami*, or a living human god.

In three works inspired by an attempted coup that took place on February 26, 1936 ("Patriotism," *Voices of the Heroic Dead*, and *Tenth-Day Chrysanthemum*), Yukio comes across with a very clear statement: it is very unfortunate that the Emperor had to become a human being. That is his core lament, his song of sadness. That is the heart of what Yukio stood for, and that is what carried him to his death. Without that, he would not have died. He would be a rich man, probably a Nobel Prize winner, worshipped for his many abilities, but this one thing got in the way. Just this one thing. And those famous lines come from Yukio's innermost self:

> Nadote sumerogi wa hito to naritamaishi,
> (Why did the Emperor have to make himself a mere human being?)
> Nadote sumerogi wa hito to naritamaishi,
> (Why did the Emperor have to make himself a mere human being?)
> Nadote sumerogi wa hito to naritamaishi"
> (Why did the Emperor have to make himself a mere human being?) [1]

This is a very, very powerful expression. And Yukio meant that to be remembered.

WHAT IS THE NATIONAL ENTITY OF JAPAN?

On the day of the state funeral for Showa Tenno, I went to visit one man. I just wanted to spend some time with him, just sit there, knowing that he had the same attitude as me. He's a very well-known Japanese businessman. He's very well known. He and I sat there and we recited those famous lines, "*Nadote sumerogi wa hito to naritamaishi.*" Even with my poor knowledge of Japanese, I felt the power of those words. The man in question was quite close with Yukio and a very sophisticated, amusing man; he is still alive in Azabu. He received me in his study. I can't remember how I arranged this, but I must have called him at home. I had his telephone number. He knew me, and he knew that I had known Yukio, and he respected me for that. I haven't seen him since that day. The emotional atmosphere was so highly charged. I sat with him and recited those famous lines. Edward George Seidensticker, well known for his translation of *The Tale of Genji* as well as of Mishima's works, was also interested in those famous lines. But I didn't want to go and recite them with Seidensticker. He is another *gaijin* like me.

I wanted to hear the voice and look at the face of someone who understood. It was raining on that day. I went to the businessman's house, by appointment of course, and knocked on the door. He took me into his little study. He's a poet and has many books. This was Seiji Tsutsumi (he passed away soon after the Japanese version of this book was first published and became a bestseller in Japan). He understood Yukio's writings. And Yukio himself reported to me that there is only one respectable businessman, this man, in Japan. Tsutsumi-san was one interesting person. He created the Sezon Museum of Art in Ikebukuro. His interest in contemporary art coincided with mine. I knew him as a poet, an artist, and a cultural organizer, not as a businessman. His brother, the owner of the Seibu Railway, was a very difficult man. His father, also difficult, was known as "Pistol" Tsutsumi. Seiji's mother was very important in his life and she came into the compound on that day. I saw her there at some point. But it's easier to appreciate Mishima through that little event on that important day. It's easier to appreciate him as a mover and shaker.

Tony (Hideaki) Kase is convinced that Mishima was an unsatisfactory person. He wrote in *Shokun*, an opinion magazine published by *Bungei* Shunju, that the *Tatenokai* (Shield Society) uniform was like the costume worn by doormen at cabarets in Ginza. I think he believes that Mishima made a fool of Yamashita, the chief at the Ichigaya Headquarters of the Ground Self-Defense Force's Eastern Army, and talked his way into the office and tied him up. Tony is critical of those actions, and says if Yukio was seriously planning a coup d'état, he should have occupied the office of the Defense Agency Chief, which was in Roppongi. But there was no balcony, and aluminum windows do not provide the appropriate theatrical setting.

Nonetheless, I feel that what Yukio insisted on in his manifesto is not so much different from what Tony has proclaimed throughout his career as a conservative critic. Tony does not, perhaps, agree with Yukio's method. Both, however, share the same view: Japan must wrest its *kokutai* (national entity) as a sovereign nation, with a long history with the Emperor at its pinnacle, from the control exerted by the victorious nations of WWII.

The Imperial Japanese Army's officers and soldiers went to war, and at the conflict's final stage, resorted to having young soldiers fight as *Tokkotai* (suicide attack force). They fought to protect their *kokutai* and their living human god, the Tenno. I strongly believe that Yukio opted to sacrifice his own life to express his ideas in his own language. Yukio had something worth protecting even by sacrificing his own life.

Foreigners have tried to understand Yukio and his value judgments in their own ways. Yukio expressed his values in the form of literature so that they would be easier for people to understand, and then took the actions that he took as another way of expressing himself.

Yukio was a serious person. He expressed his ideas in writing as an outstanding novelist, a candidate for the Nobel Prize for literature. Then he expressed himself through his actions. Yukio was a man who subjectively lived a life nobody else could lead. There is no one like Yukio. Novels are like reality and reality is like novels. Such was the world of Yukio Mishima. At his height, he surpassed the world of ideology. Yukio made the world of reality and the world of imagination coexist.

Yukio noticed that Japan had wonderful treasures which other countries did not possess. Yukio was not a typical Japanese. He was a pure Japanese, but was influenced by Western culture. His actions were in accord with the spirit that is unique to Japanese culture. Yukio, who possessed a patriotic personality, and was moved by the *Tokkotai*'s pure mentality of love for their country. He was proud of the *Tokkotai*.

The divinity of the Tenno is an important topic. The Imperial Navy and Army officers and soldiers, *Tokkotai* members, who sacrificed their lives for the sake of their own country, all believed that the Emperor was a divine being. Therefore, they felt obligated to risk their lives to protect him. That's the core of Japan. Without a divine emperor, Japan is not really Japan. I truly believe that Mishima advanced that line of thinking in a most convincing way.

There are various ways in which foreign eyes see this tradition, but Mishima made it easy to understand. I am sure people understand that the difference between someone who gave up everything—his reputation, his family, his money, his work, his excitement about being Japanese . . . Yukio sacrificed so much. In *The New York Times* over the last twenty years, my colleagues have denounced Nakasone, Shintaro Ishihara, and Tony for their right-wing views, but what have those men actually given up? What sacrifices have they made? I asked my friend who succeeded me as bureau chief at *The New York Times* in Tokyo: "Why are you scared of Ishihara? He's a playboy. He wouldn't sacrifice a tiny piece of his finger for his country. So how can you denounce him as a right-winger? He's nothing of the kind." But young *Tokkotai* members and Mishima were the genuine article. Yukio inherited the spirit of Shoin Yoshida. He adored that side of Japan. And so do I.

Speaking of Shoin Yoshida, Yukio felt that the man was brave enough to confront the foreign invaders, to try to get on one of their ships so he could go to America. Once there he would study and learn about that country, and then come back to Japan. Of course, he was arrested. But he continued to create trouble from the authorities' point of view, and was eventually executed. It's a very sad part of Japanese history that this man and others like him, who were prepared to and did sacrifice everything, are not seen as the major figures they were. I think there was something in Yukio that made him say to himself, "This is really a shame. Yoshida should have been recognized." There's a little shrine in Shimoda and that's about it. I don't recall, I am ashamed to say, what conversations Yukio and I had about Yoshida, but there is a chapter in Ivan Morris' book on Japanese heroes. It's a very worthwhile text.[2]

Yukio felt that the uniqueness of this country lay in certain predominant features. His attitude toward patriots was that they had served their country to the absolute highest level. Yukio was very proud of them, and felt that no foreigner would ever really understand this part of Japanese thinking, with the exception of somebody like Ivan Morris. Seidensticker translated the *Decay of the Angel* (*Tennin gosui*), one part of Yukio's *Sea of Fertility* (*Hojo no umi*) tetralogy, but he was not particularly close to Yukio. I think Keene was much closer. Morris dedicated his great work on Japanese heroes to Yukio. There isn't a separate chapter on Mishima because Ivan wasn't really ready to write it. I was, but he wasn't.

Yukio perhaps thought I would understand. Yes, I have no doubt about that. My understanding is, as I have endlessly said, that he sacrificed everything. And what the politicians of that era, Sato and Nakasone, had to say wasn't very important. They dismissed Yukio as mad. Of course, he was mad. He had to become insane to do what he did.

WRITING *LIFE AND DEATH OF YUKIO MISHIMA*

It was incredibly hard for me to write *Life and Death of Yukio Mishima*, especially Chapter 1, because the book had to be a literal description of what happened: it had to be literally true, factually accurate. On the other hand, proceeding with only the facts, it is very difficult to write about the death of someone you know. You have to go mad, as it were. You have to become crazy in order to attempt the task of describing this work for Mishima. I struggled with this for a couple of years. And I knew that if I couldn't progress past the death scene, I would never be able to complete this book. In fact, I saw that there was a good chance I would never finish, because it was just too much for me to take on.

The shock of what happened was really huge. But as the one and only foreign journalist who spent time with him, I just had to write. Just before he committed suicide, I received a letter, handwritten in English, by Yukio, in which he mentioned "the end of the world."

Dear Henry:

Enclosed are copies of my essay and short-story, which, I hope, might interest you.

I am still occupied by writing the last volume.

Finishing a long novel makes me feel sometimes as if it will be the end of the world.

As always,

Yukio Mishima (4 Oct, 1970)

Yukio had placed his faith in me in some way, maybe in a very small way. Small is big in this case. I felt I had a responsibility. I didn't go around telling people that, but that's what I felt.

My wife Akiko departed for Paris for her art studies and I stayed in Switzerland in a chalet by myself. It was a big chalet on the lake in Zurich. I had my typewriter—you used typewriters in those days, and I put it to work. It didn't come out right. I kept writing descriptions that were either boring or untrue. Finally, one afternoon, I was working. And the same facts lined themselves up. There was no change in the facts, of course. But one afternoon—I wasn't drunk, I wasn't drugged, I didn't use anything except a couple of cups of coffee—one afternoon, it just wrote itself, as if an invisible hand or an invisible head was doing the job. Something took over. Something worked. Forty pages or so of manuscript that day came out right.

As I looked out at the mountains surrounding this chalet in a small Swiss town, I saw apple trees a nearby slope. They started to dance. What happened to me had happened in a way to Vincent van Gogh when he got caught up in his landscapes in Provence. Vincent van Gogh's experience isn't difficult to understand if you are already halfway there. But being visited with such an experience is pretty tough, and it doesn't happen to human beings often.

For a couple of hours, I watched the trees. It seemed to me that it was a couple of hours or so; I can revisit that experience. It could have been a couple of minutes. God, I saw the trees dancing and shaking. It just seemed very normal. Those were the circumstances under which I could proceed. I never touched that text again—I never changed a word.

In the early 1980s I was writing a column on the Imperial Family and the Emperor's succession. At that time I learned that the Emperor had not visited Yasukuni Shrine since 1975. So I made an inquiry to the Imperial Household Agency, the Kunaicho. The reply: after 1975 Emperor Showa did not visit Yasukuni Shrine even once, up until his death. The current Emperor has not visited Yasukuni Shrine since he came to the throne. I didn't make any further inquiry. I just wrote the facts. I didn't ask for the rationale because it was a touchy issue.

Prime ministers' visits to Yasukuni Shrine took place without any opposition until the regime of Kakuei Tanaka. They became an issue during Takeo Miki's administration. Miki visited Yasukuni and said that it was a private visit and not an official one, when asked by the Kyodo News. Since then, the media has asked whether the visit was private or official whenever a prime minister or other Cabinet minister visits Yasukuni Shrine. In Western society, there is no fool who asks whether it is private or official when politicians pray in church. We do not distinguish between a private or official act when praying in front of God.

Prime Minister Yasuhiro Nakasone made it his policy to clear postwar politics of its negative inheritance. He made eleven pilgrimages to Yasukuni Shrine between 1982, his first year in office, and 1985, including annual pilgrimages on August 15. Because of Chinese protests, Nakasone's visit to Yasukuni on August 15, 1985 was his final one as prime minister. The next prime minister who visited Yasukuni was Junichiro Koizumi, some twenty years later.

It is difficult for the Emperor to visit Yasukuni Shrine when there is controversy over prime ministers' visits. Yasukuni is a place in which the spirits of fallen war heroes are enshrined. For the Emperor no occasion is private. It is so regrettable that no emperor has visited Yasukuni since 1975.

MacArthur regarded Yasukuni as a symbol of militarism and nationalism. He tried to burn it down and build a dog-racing track over it. He changed his mind because he received a letter from the Vatican's ambassador to Japan, Father Bruno Vittel. The letter warned that it is an accepted custom to respect those who died for their nation, regardless of whether that nation won or lost the war. It was a national duty as well as a national right. If Yasukuni Shrine were burnt down, that would be a criminal act that would leave a stain of extreme dishonor on American history.

If Father Vittel were alive now, what would he think about those who oppose the Yasukuni visits? If his statue were erected within the premises of Yasukuni Shrine, then people of Christian nations, such as America, Canada, Australia, and European countries would have a much better perspective.

Enshrinement of the so-called Class-A war criminals is raised as a problem. It is worthy to note that in 1952, the Japan Attorney's Alliance submitted an opinion paper to the government on the remissions for war criminals. It was the trigger of a nationwide movement. In July 1955, the bill for remission passed the Diet—426 members voted in favor of the bill. Henceforth there were no war criminals in Japan. It is either an act of negligence or repudiation of the Diet for major Japanese newspapers to say that Class-A war criminals are enshrined in Yasukuni. They are saying that "Japanese democracy is strange" and are denying the will of the Diet.

Emperor Showa said, "They may be war criminals to enemy countries, but they are the ones who devoted themselves to our country." Even though so-called Class-A war criminals are enshrined there, it is not right that the Emperor cannot visit Yasukuni Shrine because of that. That shouldn't happen. Journalists should stop asking stupid questions about whether something is private or official, to politicians visiting Yasukuni Shrine. It is important to create an atmosphere that makes it possible for anyone to freely visit Yasukuni Shrine.

I am also concerned about those people whose whereabouts became unknown. The brother of my wife's mother was on board a commercial ocean vessel during the war. Contact at sea was lost. My wife's grandmother sometimes sat on the seashore and watched the horizon for a long time, waiting for her son to come home. They never found any trace of him. My family believes his spirit came back to Yasukuni Shrine.

THE MESSAGE IN MISHIMA'S MANIFESTO

Ian Buruma, a Dutch journalist who currently resides in America, is my rival in a way, as both of us have written about Yukio Mishima. In his Mishima piece, Ian commented that the artist chose the wrong path, referring to Yukio's path toward death. He says Mishima started heading in the wrong direction after he started talking about the nation. Ian came to Japan in 1975, after Yukio's death. He never met Yukio.

Yukio never took the wrong path. Everything he did—talking about the status quo of Japan's politics, as well as writing his various novels—built up toward the end of his life; its finale was the Ichigaya incident. Yukio's main theme was to defend Japan's tradition and culture, such as the Tenno and *miyabi* (grace).

Voices of the Heroic Dead was a vow from his soul. I called my wife's mother *Obaa-san* (Grandma). I lived with her close to thirty years till her death. *Obaa-san* was always interested in Yukio. She told me, "It will take another two or three hundred years for people to understand what you are saying about Mishima."

Mishima is recognized for his novels in the West, but his critiques and political activities are beyond the focus of attention. The image of Mishima I describe is not understood internationally. *Obaa-san* may be right. I might have to wait another two or three hundred years for the time to arrive when people understand how I feel about Yukio Mishima.

What Yukio said in his *gekibun* (manifesto) is right. That's what I think and how I feel. But this view is totally lacking, in trying to understand Yukio Mishima, in Western society.

When Yukio stood on the balcony of the main building in the Ground Self-Defense Force Ichigaya Base (current location of the Defense Ministry) and called for the uprising of the SDF soldiers, he referred to the SDF as America's mercenaries. French Foreign Legion troops are European mercenaries. Mercenaries are soldiers who work for money. Proud soldiers cannot be hired for money. I would like to convey the message of Yukio's manifesto and his vow as they appear in my book *The Life and Death of Yukio Mishima*. The book was translated into Japanese by (then) *Mainichi Shimbun* reporter Takao Tokuoka, and published in Japan.

I would like the reader to read aloud with me:

> Shortly before midday, Morita, a squat figure, appeared on the balcony, followed by Ogawa. The two students came out of one of the windows of Mashita's office and walked toward the front of the balcony carrying papers and cloths in their hands.
>
> The balcony was large. It was thirty feet from the windows of the general's office to the front of the balcony.
>
> The students, with the ends of their hachimaki (headbands) trailing over their yellow-brown uniforms, came up to the parapet. Leaning over the edge of the balcony, they threw out long cotton streamers, facing the crowd. They fastened the banners to the parapet so that they dangled over the parade ground; on them were written conditions under which General Mashita's safety was guaranteed.
>
> One of the conditions was that Mishima's speech would be heard in silence. However, the noise at that moment was tremendous. Soldiers shouted excitedly at one another. Police bikes, cars, and ambulances were all running their engines on the parade ground. And more cars were arriving all the time, including press vehicles flying company pennants. The helicopters made the most noise as they came in close to film the scene.
>
> The two Tatenokai (Shield Society) students were dropping papers over the edge of the balcony on the crowd below. Some of the papers were caught by the light breeze and drifted out over the parade ground.
>
> The papers were copies of Mishima's gekibun, his last manifesto, a document modeled on statements made by rebel army officers in the numerous abortive coup d'états of the 1930's in Japan.

The gekibun read (as I have condensed it from two thousand words):

> We, members of the Tatenokai, have been handsomely treated by the Jieitai (Self-Defense Force). Why are we biting the hand that fed us?
>
> It is simply because we revere the Jieitai. The Armed Forces are the soul of Nippon.
>
> We have seen the Jieitai treated like a toy by the nation's leaders. And thus the Jieitai protects the very instrument which denies its right to exist: the Peace Constitution (the Constitution of 1947, drafted by the Allied Powers).
>
> Opportunities to rectify this dreadful error have been missed. On October 21, 1969, the Jieitai should have been mobilized and thrown into the battle against anti-war demonstrators. The Jieitai should then have taken power and demanded revision of the Constitution.
>
> The chance was missed. The honor of the nation is at stake. The Jieitai is unconstitutional, and no steps are being taken to save it. [Mishima was referring to Article 9 of the Constitution, according to which Japan will "never maintain armed forces.]

Our fundamental values, as Japanese, are threatened. The Emperor is not being given his rightful place in Japan.

We have waited in vain for the Jieitai to rebel. If no action is taken, the Western powers will control Japan for the next century.

The manifesto ended with this appeal:

Let us restore Nippon to its true state and let us die. Will you value only life and let the spirit die? . . . We will show you a value which is greater than respect for life. Not liberty, not democracy. It is Nippon! Nippon, the land of history and tradition. The Japan we love.

The soldiers on the parade ground picked up copies of the gekibun. Some read the document. Others stuffed the papers into their pockets. The men were puzzled. Most of them were young and had had no experience of the war. For twenty-five years Japan had been at peace, and the alliance with America, the cornerstone of Japanese foreign policy, had been challenged only by the left. Nothing had prepared these young men for this assault from the right. Many of them knew of the existence of the Tatenokai, but they had no notion of its purpose. Nor did they understand why Mishima—a famous novelist—had involved himself in this enterprise. Adding to their bafflement was the spectacle of wounded men being carried from the building. Why had Mishima attacked and injured their officers?

At midday precisely, Mishima himself appeared on the balcony. He strode forward to the front of the balcony, a small figure in the yellow-brown uniform of the Tatenokai.

The men below saw only his head, with a hachimaki bound around it, the symbol of the Rising Sun in the center of the forehead.

He leapt up onto the parapet. His small, wiry frame came entirely into view. The buttons of his uniform gleamed brightly in the November sun. He wore white gloves on which bloodstains were visible.

He braced himself, shoulders back, his hands on his hips.

Tenno Heika Banzai!

"It is a wretched affair," Mishima began, "to have to speak to Jieitai men in circumstances like these."

The helicopters were making a great noise. Many in the crowd could not hear Mishima's words.

"I thought," Mishima continued, "that the Jieitai was the last hope of Nippon, the last stronghold of the Japanese soul."

His words were blotted out by the helicopters.

"But . . . . Japanese people today think of money, just money. Where is our national spirit today? The politicians care nothing for Japan. They are greedy for power.

"The Jieitai," Mishima continued, "must be the soul of Nippon. The soldiers! The army!"

"But . . . . we were betrayed by the Jieitai!"

There were shouts from the crowd.

"Cut it out now!"

"Bakayaro!" (An untranslatable swear word.)

"Arse-hole!"

Mishima grew excited. "Listen! Listen! Hear me out! Listen! Listen! Listen to me!"

He resumed. "We thought that the Jeitai was the soul of national honor!"

There were shouts.

"Come down from there!"

"We don't agree with you!"

Mishima went on. "The nation has no spiritual foundation. That is why you don't agree with me! You don't understand Japan. The Jieitai must put things right!"

There was violent hooting.

"Listen!" shouted Mishima. "Be quiet, will you! Listen!"

"Bakayaro!"

Mishima tried to go on.

"Kiss your arse," shouted a soldier below.

"Don't you hear!" Mishima shouted back. "I ask you to be quiet! Listen! Hear me out!"

"Stop playing the hero!" another heckler shouted.

"Just listen to me!" Mishima hurled back. "What happened last year? On October 21? There was a demonstration, an anti-war demonstration. On October 21 last year. In Shinjuku. And the police put it down. The police! After that there was, and there will be, no chance to amend the Constitution."

"So what?"

"So the Jiminto [the Liberal Democratic Party], the politicians, decided that they could just use the police. The police would deal with the demonstration. Don't you see?"

"Hooray. Call the police. Dial 110, somebody!"

Mishima fought on. "Look! The government did not use the Jieitai. The Armed Forces stayed in their barracks. The Constitution is fixed forever. There will be no chance to amend it. Do you understand?"

"No, no. Absolutely not!"

"No, we don't follow you."

"No!"

"All right," Mishima said, "Listen! Since last October 21, since that time, it is you who protect the Constitution. The Jieitai defends the Constitution. There will be no chance to amend it. Not for twenty years! The Jieitai waited for that chance, with tears in their eyes. Too late!"

"Japan is at peace!"

Mishima looked at his watch. He had been speaking for less than five minutes.

"Why don't you understand? Think about October 21 last year! Since that time I have waited for the Jieitai to act! When would the Jieitai come to its senses? I waited. There will be no further chance to revise the Constitution! The Jieitai will never become an army! It has no foundation, no center!"

"The Jieitai must rise. Why?" he went on.

"Come down! Come down!"

"To protect Japan! You must protect Japan! To protect Japan! Yes, to protect Japan! Japanese tradition! Our history! Our culture! The Emperor!

His audience exploded with shouts and jeers.

"Listen! Listen! Listen! Listen!"

"A man appeals to you! A man! I am staking my life on this! Do you hear? Do you follow me? If you do not rise with me, if the Jieitai will not rise, the Constitution will never be amended!" He paused. "You will be just American mercenaries. American troops!"

"*Bakayaro!*"

"Stop talking!"

"Come down!"

Mishima could scarcely make himself heard above the din.

"I have waited for four years! Yes, four years! I wanted the Jieitai to rise! Four years!"

"I have come to the last thirty minutes," he said. "Yes, the last thirty minutes. I am waiting. I want . . . "

His words were lost in the noise of helicopter engines.

"Are you *bushi*? Are you men? You *are* soldiers? Then why do you stand by the Constitution? You back the Constitution that denies your very existence!"

There were mock cries of alarm from the crowd.

"Then you have no future!" roared Mishima. "You will never be saved! It is the end. The Constitution will remain forever. You are finished!"

He hammered the point. "You are unconstitutional! Listen! You are all unconstitutional!"

There was no reaction from the crowd.

"Don't you understand? Don't you see what is happening? Don't you understand that it is you who defend the Constitution? Why not? Why don't you understand? I have been waiting for you. Why don't you wake up? There you are in your tiny world. You do nothing for Nippon!"

"Is that why you injured our men?"

"They put up a resistance."

"Don't be stupid! What do you mean by 'resistance'?"

Once more Mishima appealed to the men. "Will any of you rise with me?" He waited ten seconds.

"Bakayaro!"

"Who would rise with you?"

"Madman!"

"No one?" Mishima asked.

"Are you a man?"

"You say that! Have you studied *Bushido* [the warrior ethic]? Do you understand the way of the sword? What does the sword mean to a Japanese? . . . I ask you. Are *you* men?"

Mishima's voice grew calmer. "I see that you are not. You will not rise. You will do nothing. The Constitution means nothing to you. You are not interested."

"I have lost my dream of the Jieitai!" he added.

"Come down!"

"Drag him down from there!"

"Why does no one stop him?"

"Bakayaro!"

Most of the crowd looked on in silence as the sporadic heckling continued.

"I salute the Emperor!" cried Mishima.

"Tenno Heika Banzai! Tenno Heika Banzai! Tenno Heika Banzai!"

As he shouted this traditional salute ("Long live the Emperor! Long live the Emperor! Long live the Emperor!"), Morita, who had been standing behind him—only his head visible to the men below—joined in. The two *Tatenokai* leaders raised their hands thrice as they shouted.

"Shoot him!"

"SHOOT HIM!"

Mishima jumped down from the parapet onto the balcony behind it. With Morita at his heels, he retraced his steps to the general's office. He stooped at the low window and went down into the room beyond, out of sight of the TV cameras. Then Morita, too, disappeared. The window was closed.[3]

I heard from Yukio that he had decided to organize *Tatenokai* after he finished writing *Voices of the Heroic Dead*. Japan's *kokutai* or national entity has the Tenno, who is a living human god, at its center. The role of the army, especially in the form of the Imperial Army, is to protect the *kokutai*.

Yukio did not say much, but he tried to show the existence of something which is more precious than life through his action. Being an outstanding writer, Yukio expressed himself not in language but in sacrificing his life. That was, in fact, the only way for him to express his ideas.

THE STATUS QUO OF A FAKE SOVEREIGN COUNTRY, JAPAN

I just read aloud my own description of Yukio's appeal at Ichigaya. Japan hasn't amended its constitution yet.

Japan is still under occupation. Sovereignty has not been restored. For me, Japan looks like a part of America, or like a miserable protectorate. As Yukio expressed in his *gekibun*, the Self-Defense Force has become America's mercenary, merely support troops. Truly a joke. How should we regard what happened in Ichigaya? Perhaps it was a call to action that ended in failure.

When you read Yukio's appeal, how do you feel about what both sides said? Which side do you support, Mishima or the Jieitai members? Indeed, it was a battle between mercenaries for a foreign power (the SDF) and a real Japanese, Yukio Mishima. Yukio called for an uprising by the SDF, in vain. The SDF didn't respond, and Yukio's appeal failed.

But because Yukio sacrificed his life, this incident is still mentioned and discussed. Yukio selected death to allow his soul to live forever. I can understand what Yukio tried to insist on. The message was to revise the mercenary status, to amend the Constitution, which denies the existence of the SDF, and to protect the existence of the Tenno as the living, human god! I can understand such objectives.

Yukio's last message was not radical at all, except that he unrealistically attempted a coup d'état. Is an attempt to amend the Constitution, forced upon Japan by America during the Occupation (Japan did not have sovereignty at that time) in order to prevent Japan from becoming an independent state, radical? Is it radical to restore the status of the Tenno, which well reflects Japanese culture? England is not England without its royal institution. Is Japan without the Tenno really Japan?

Without an army, an independent nation will not survive. The SDF, however, is fraudulent. Unless Japan amends the "protectorate" Constitution and identifies the SDF as a national army, Japan is a sovereign state in name only.

Japan became a bizarre nation, throwing away its tradition and history. English people respect English tradition and history. People who visit England will feel that in the political entity called England, the past is alive in the present. Yukio, of course, knew that thorough preparation was necessary in order for his coup d'état to be a success. To awaken the Japanese people, he staged a drama by actually committing suicide.

NOTES

1. Mishima Yukio, Eirei no koe (Voices of the heroic dead) (Tokyo: Kawade Shobo Shinsha, 1966).

2. Ivan Morris, The Nobility of Failure: Tragic Heroes in the History of Japan (Austin: Holt, Rinehart and Winston, 1975).

3. Scott Stokes, Henry. *The Life and Death of Yukio Mishima* . Cooper Square Press, 2000.

Chapter Seven

Japan as the Light of Hope for Asia

THE 60ᵀᴴ ANNIVERSARY OF THE RESTORATION
OF DIPLOMATIC RELATIONS BETWEEN JAPAN AND INDIA

In December 2012, the 60ᵗʰ Anniversary of the Restoration of Diplomatic Relations between Japan and India was commemorated at the Bunkyo Civic Hall near Tokyo Dome in Korakuen Amusement Park. The event was held by an organization which promotes democracy in the region of Asia, and whose slogan is "Free Asia."

In addition to the representative from India, representatives and supporters from Tibet, Uygur, Southern Mongolia, Taiwan, and North Korea gathered together. Many wore traditional costumes from their mother countries.

I was the keynote speaker; the title of my speech was "Japan as the Light of Hope for Asia." The speech was in English; we had a Japanese translation projected using PowerPoint. It was a "simultaneous translation," with written statements rather than simultaneous oral interpretation. While I was giving my 40-minute English speech, I worried that everyone who didn't understand English might fall asleep just reading written statements in Japanese. But it was a needless fear. At the end of my speech, it seemed as though the applause would never cease, and I was given a standing ovation. Many people came up to me and said, "It was a marvelous speech." Allow me to present the text of my speech:

Good evening, ladies and gentlemen. My name is Henry Stokes. Thank you for inviting me to speak to you today.

This symposium is held to celebrate the 60ᵗʰ anniversary of the establishment of diplomatic relations between Japan and India in 1952. I am very honored to be able to participate in this historic moment.

79

One of the most surprising developments in the 20th century has been the sheer speed at which the 500-year curse of colonialism came to an end. Rule by white men petered out in mid-air. No one seems to have expected this.

Nehru, when asked in the late 1930s how long he thought it would take for India to gain its independence, ventured the opinion that it might come in the 1970s. In other words, after his time! By the early 1940s, it was becoming obvious that the Indians themselves were not going to be patient that long. What had happened to change all expectations?

The simple answer is the Second World War had broken out and it showed a relative newcomer to the world stage in the 500-year drama, capable of delivering enormous blows to colonialism. And that was Japan. Thus, the Nehru timetable of independence for India by the 1970s gave way to a much tighter timetable, namely as soon as World War Two ended.

Let us go back in time from the 20th century to the early 17th century.

In India, Britain established the East India Company in 1600 and started their colonial rule. Britain further branched out its East India Company to Madras in 1637, to Bombay in 1661, and to Calcutta in 1690. The British Invasion continued with these landmark events: the Battle of Plassey in 1764, the Mysore War in 1799, and the Sikh Revolt in 1845. The famous Sepoy Revolt took place from 1857 till 1859. It was an anti-British civilian rebellion.

In the midst of the UK oppression of India, the Meiji Restoration took place in Japan in 1868. In India, at roughly that same time, some historical figures in the struggle for Indian independence were born:

Mahatma Gandhi was born in 1867. And Chandra Bose in 1897.

In 1877, the British Indian Empire, featuring direct colonial rule of the whole of India by the British, was founded. And Queen Victoria came to the throne as the "Empress of India." In other words, Bose was born at the peak of British colonial rule of India.

Bose is called "Netaji" in India even now. Netaji means "great leader." With Japan's support, Bose formed the INA—the Indian National Army. Unlike Gandhi who fought against British colonial rule using a non-violence philosophy, Bose fought in battle as a commander.

On May 16, 1943, Bose came to Japan and met Japanese leaders: Navy Minister Shimada, Chief of Navy General Staff Nagano, Foreign Minister Shigemitsu. And then he met the Prime Minister, Hideki Tojo. Bose gave his address at Hibiya Public Hall. His message summed up the feeling of Asian people at that time.

He said, "When I started elementary school, a country of an Asian race fought against one of the world's largest white empires, Russia. This Asian country defeated Russia completely. And this country was Japan. When this news reached all across India, a wave of excitement covered the entire land. At every corner of my country, people enthusiastically talked about the Battle of Port Arthur, the Battle of Mukden, and the thrilling story of the Battle of Tsushima. Indian children honestly adored Admiral Togo and General Nogi. Parents competed to buy pictures of Admiral Togo and General Nogi, in vain. Instead, they bought something Japanese from the market and ornamented their houses with Japanese things."

Bose clearly said, "Japan was the 'Light of Hope' for Asia." He further continued, "This time, Japan declared war against Britain, a long time enemy of India. Japan has given us the best opportunity to be independent. We realize its significance and thank Japan from the bottom of our hearts. Once we miss this opportunity, we would not be able to have the same opportunity for another 100 years or more. Victory is in our hands and we firmly believe India will accomplish our goal of being independent."

What really counted was action, not talk. In October of 1943, which was the 66th year since Queen Victoria came to throne as the Empress of India, the Provisional Government of Free India was established. At a Convention held in Singapore, Bose was nominated to be the head by unanimous applause.

Bose declared, "Chalo Delhi" which means "On to Delhi." He and his people held up a board on which the same message was written and marched in the street. It was a historical start of the march heading for their homeland India. INA or Indian National Army officers and soldiers, together with the Japanese Army, heading for Imphal, passing the border of Burma and India, shouting, "On to Delhi." Bose encouraged officers and soldiers saying, "Raise our national flag on the Red Fort!"

The Provisional Government of Free India, together with Japan, declared war against Britain and America. In the fall of the same year, 1943, the Greater East Asian Conference was held from November 5 to 6 in Tokyo. This was the first Summit of the colored races held for the first time in the long history of humanity.

Prime Minister Hideki Tojo of Japan met leaders from other Asian countries: Zhang Jinghui (Prime Minister of Manchuria), Wang Jingwei (Chairman of the Nanking Government of China), Jose P. Laurel (President of The Philippines), Ba Maw (Prime Minister of Burma), Prince Wan Waithayakon (Acting Prime Minister of Thailand) gathered together. And Subhas Chandra Bose attended as a representative of India.

Today not a few Japanese scholars regard this conference as if it were the gathering of the Japanese military's "puppet government" leaders for propaganda purposes. But the Japanese who say such a thing are the "puppets" of foreign powers which intend to control the minds of the Japanese people.

At the Conference, the Greater East Asian Joint Declaration was approved unanimously. Bose appealed, "I pray to God that this Joint Declaration . . . may prove to be a charter for the nations of East Asia and what is more, a charter for the suppressed nations of the whole world. May this Joint Declaration be the new charter of liberty . . . ." As Bose proclaimed, Japan was "the Light of Hope" for non-white people of the world.

World history of the past 500 years is a grand drama, of the Western Powers of white Christians ruling the nations of colored races, as their colonies. In such a historical context, Japan is an unprecedented nation. It is worthy to note that Japan proposed abolition of racial discrimination at the Paris Conference held right after WWI. At this conference, the post-war order of the world, including the foundation of the League of Nations, was discussed. When a proposal for abolition of racial discrimination was presented, Prime Minister Hughes of White Australia left the conference room, saying he would refuse signing such a proposal and go home.

The Chairman was US President Woodrow Wilson. He demanded that the Japanese representative withdraw this proposal, saying that the matter was an issue which should be treated quietly. Baron Nobuaki Makino, the chief Japanese representative and a former Japanese Foreign Minister, would not follow Chairman Wilson's demand and requested a vote.

Although Britain, America, Poland, Brazil and Rumania were opposed, 11 countries, mostly minor, out of the attending 16 countries voted for the Japanese proposal. Thus the proposal won by a majority and was approved. Nonetheless, Chairman Wilson, the US President, announced that the voting itself was invalid because it was not a "unanimous vote." Makino still demanded that the conference accept the majority vote, but Wilson insisted that "important issues like this one required a solid vote in the past. At least no objection is needed to proceed with the meeting."

Despite the fact that the proposal for abolishing racial discrimination was approved by an overwhelming majority of 11 to 5, Chairman Wilson, the US president, ignored the result of the vote. Such behavior would be unacceptable in today's civilized world. Today, the President of the United States is black, but such a thing would have been totally unbelievable back then. The Japanese are not white, they are a colored people. So the proud Japanese were not able to overlook such high-handedness by whites.

In Indonesia, colonial rule began when the Dutch dispatched their navy to Indonesia in 1596. Three hundred and fifty years or so of colonial rule by the Dutch ended in 1942 when the Japanese army advanced to Indonesia. The Dutch Army surrendered in only 7 days. An Indonesian legend has it that God's soldiers led by a hero riding a white horse helped Indonesia to become independent. Japan's advance reminded Indonesian people of the coming of those legendary soldiers of God. The Japanese Army was the Army of the Myth.

Dr. George Hu'eu Sanford Kanahele raises 4 points as to Japan's role in his thesis entitled The Japanese Occupation of Indonesia: Prelude to Independence.

Banned the use of Dutch and English. Due to this, Indonesian spread as the official language.

Gave military training to Indonesian youth. Thus young Indonesian people learned strict rules, endurance and courage.

Swept away the Dutch authorities and gave high posts to Indonesians. This improved Indonesian's ability and responsibility.

Established Putra (as a civil organization) and Hoko-kai (a voluntary service society) in Java and built its network and chapters across the country. The Japanese taught Indonesians how to operate these nationwide network organizations.

It is widely said that Japan invaded Asian countries during WWII. But if so how come the invaded country provided military training to the youth of the country being invaded, encouraged them to enhance their mental abilities, gave them high positions, helped them build nationwide organizations, and taught them how to manage such organizations?

These facts certainly prove that Japan was not the country which invaded Indonesia. It is correct to say that Japan made all efforts possible to let Asian countries be independent. Independent from whom?

Of course, from the rule of Western countries which colonized Asian countries. At the center of Jakarta is Merdeka Square. Merdeka means "independence" in Indonesia. Besides raising statues of Hatta and Sukarno, the

Indonesians raised a 137-meter-tall Memorial Tower of Independence. On the first level there is the original statement of the Declaration of Independence on which we can find the signature of Hatta and Sukarno. On this document, Independence Day is recorded as 17-8-'05.

17-8 means August 17, the date of Independence. But what about '05, meaning the Year 5? Many Indonesians are Muslim, but it is not reference to an Islamic calendar. Needless to say, it is not a Christian calendar. Then what is this '05, the fifth year?

The Year Five, '05, in fact, refers to the Japanese Imperial Calendar. The year 1945 is, according to the Japanese Imperial Calendar, the 2605th year since the first Emperor Jimmu came to the Imperial throne and officially founded Japan. Hatta and Sukarno used Japan's Imperial Calendar to express their gratitude to Japan, for Japan was the mother of Indonesia's independence. Thus they used Japan's Imperial Calendar to celebrate their day of independence in their Declaration of Independence document.

Ladies and gentlemen, this tale we have told of 500 years of colonialism is widely known all over the world. Nonetheless, we are gathered today to celebrate the end of the curse of colonialism.

Japan is the country of the Rising Sun. Joining hands together with fellow Asian people who desire a truly Free Asia, I sincerely hope that Japan will play a vital role for realizing democratic Asian unity. Hoping the sun rises again, I would like to conclude my speech tonight.

Thank you very much for your kind attention.

JAPAN MUST BE LIBERATED
FROM THE CURSE OF THE OCCUPATION

The year 2013 fell on the 70th anniversary of the Greater East Asiatic Conference held in Tokyo in 1943. It also coincided with the second administration of Prime Minister Shinzo Abe. The administration introduced "Abenomics" (economic policies advocated by Abe), and started to turn the Japanese economy around. In the Upper House election in June of the same year, the ruling Liberal Democratic Party won an overwhelming victory. In his first administration, Abe advocated breaking free from the postwar regime, and accomplished a lot in that regard, but Japan has yet to be liberated from the curse of the Occupation. Japan is still under the influence of the historical view of the Tokyo Trials. Japan was labeled as a criminal nation which was guilty of committing a "war of aggression" and the "Nanking Massacre." It is vital, therefore, to get rid of the falsehood of the "Nanking Massacre," which was imprinted on the minds of the Japanese as an American war-guilt propaganda campaign to impose a sense of guilt about the war, Chinese propaganda and the nonsensical Tokyo Trials. Japan should tell the world the facts: that Japan did not invade Asia, but liberated Asia from Western colonial rule.

As Chandra Bose declared, "Japan was the light of hope in Asia." The Japanese Army advanced into Asia and fought against the Western powers, which controlled and oppressed Asians through colonial rule. It expelled the invaders from Asia and started the construction of an Asia for the Asians. Because of that, Asian fighters for independence arose in various Asian countries. Together with those Asian fighters, Japan fought a war for the liberation of Asia.

That was the pinnacle of the Japanese race. When England fought a "lonely war," all by herself against Hitler's Germany, Churchill encouraged his nation by saying that "if the British Empire and its Commonwealth last for a thousand years, men will still say, 'This was their finest hour.'"

Today, how many of those under seventy years old know anything about the Greater East Asiatic Conference? Most Japanese know nothing about the moment when Japan's history heated up. After WWII, many Asian and African countries attained their independence. I think they did so because Japan fought the Greater East Asian War in order to construct an Asia for Asians.

The notion of breaking free from the postwar regime should be understood from that broad historical perspective in order to overcome the historical view based on the Tokyo Trials.

Chapter Eight

Asian Leaders I Have Met

1. SELF-INTEREST-DRIVEN KIM DAE-JUNG

A Chameleonic Politician

In 2000, Kim Dae-jung won the Nobel Prize for Peace. That same year he visited North Korea for the first time as president of South Korea. Kim was awarded the prize for his contributions to peace between the North and South. The question is: Did North-South Korean relations improve due to his visit? The value of the Nobel Prize for Peace is often questioned when it comes to who receive it.

President Obama also won the Peace Prize, in 2009, but this was merely nine months after he took office, enjoying unprecedented popularity. The reason he won the prize is that he called for the abolition of nuclear weapons in his speech in Berlin. He could have also called for the eradication of all diseases on earth.

In 2013 the Nobel Peace Prize was given to the OPCW (Organization for the Prohibition of Chemical Weapons), which was founded in accordance with the Chemical Weapons Convention, a worldwide treaty that bans chemical weapons. The prize won public attention, with perfect timing, as an operation to destroy chemical weapons in Syria had just begun. But we still don't know whether this operation was successful.

In the previous year, the same prize was given to the EU, the economy of which had collapsed; the EU is still in the middle of an economic crisis. In England, public opinion has shifted to support for breaking from the EU.

I interviewed Kim Dae-jung over a dozen times. He was the highest-ranking among the VIPs I met in Japan and other Asian countries. Kim was born in a small village in a province then called Jeolla; it is currently known as Jeollanam-do, in the southwestern part of South Korea. He was a man who was always especially conscious of how the media portrayed him. He was like a chameleon, tailoring his attitude and policies to whatever situation he faced. He did not join his country's own army, rather he volunteered with the Imperial Japanese Army and served for a while. During WWII, he wore the rank-and-file uniform of the Imperial Japanese Army.

He displayed himself most dramatically when he visited North Korea for the first time as the president of South Korea. He won the attention of the entire world.

Kim Dae-jung Posed as a Pro-democracy Activist

I first met Kim Dae-jung in the 1970s, when he was still in the opposition. He was promoting a democratic movement in South Korea, staying alternately in Japan and in America. He was the focus of attention as a human rights activist.

On August 8, 1973, Kim disappeared from the Hotel Grand Palace in Kudanshita, Tokyo. The KCIA (Korean Central Intelligence Agency) had abducted him. He was taken to a ship, which then left from a Japanese port. The abductors wanted to murder him, right there on the ship, at sea. Suddenly, military aircraft flew overhead, circling the ship. The abductors gave up on murdering him.

Then he was put under house arrest, and later jailed in 1976 after publishing his "Declaration of Democratic Salvation." In February 1980 his civil rights were restored, but in May he was arrested again. This became the cause of the Kwangju Incident. The Army suppressed demonstrators who demanded democracy; this led to much bloodshed.

Kim Dae-jung was extremely attentive towards America. He was against the continuing stationing of the US Army in South Korea. His protests were really aggressive, so a lot of attention was paid to him. Nobody else protested as aggressively as he did. Whenever he accepted my interview, he posed an image of himself as a fighter of the democratic movement.

In the late 1970s President Park Chung-hee was assassinated. Park was in office from 1961 till the 1970s. Immediately after his assassination, the military took control of administration. The military headquarters saw Kim Dae-jung as a key anti-army, pro-democratic leader. The Army planned to kill its enemy.

I called on Kim Dae-jung at his residence. He was under house arrest, and army security and surveillance were extremely tight. Visiting him at his residence several times as *The New York Times* correspondent, I noticed that he had a special preference for that newspaper. There was a clear difference compared to that of other news reporters. His residence was the largest in the neighborhood, and was always surrounded by media. But as soon as Kim learned about my arrival as *The New York Times* correspondent, he always let me in.

It was America that saved him. America's private organizations and media opinion backed Kim Dae-jung, and *The New York Times* was at the forefront. In the spring of 1980 I was based in Seoul, and traveled back and forth between Tokyo. Kim was at the peak of his life when I repeatedly met and interviewed him. I wrote that Kim Dae-jung was the central figure of the democratic movement in Korea. I insisted in an editorial that he not be executed, no matter what rationale was given.

The Man Who Plotted the Kwangju Uprising

But Kim Dae-jung was a fake, not a real person. He was an imposter and a pretender. He was an actor who tried at all times to take advantage of a situation by controlling people's feelings. He was not what he pretended to be. I was deceived by him, and so were many of the Korean people. He was brilliant in this respect; his act of deception was never uncovered.

Kim Dae-jung's biggest crime was that he deceived democracy. He was never criticized for this, not even once. The Kwangju Uprising made his fraud clear. In 1980 he was arrested by Chun Doo-hwan, who was at the pinnacle of the military. Kim knew, more than anybody else, that he was the wire-puller, the man behind Kwangju. What Kim Dae-jung wanted was power; what he always had in mind was his position. During the Kwangju Uprising, what he had in mind at all times was himself and seizing power.

Twenty years after the Kwangju Incident, in 2000, I compiled a book entitled *The Kwangju Uprising* as chief editor, with Lee Jae-eui, and published it with a New York publisher. Ten Western and another ten Korean journalists who reported the incident back in 1980 wrote about what happened in Kwangju at that time. Through this book, what we couldn't report at the time the uprising occurred became clear. All contributors freely wrote their recollections and experience.

Actually, the Kwangju Uprising was the "Kim Dae-jung Uprising." It was an extraordinary effort by a rising politician who planned to be president, who eventually became so, and who aimed at bettering relations with North Korea. I did not see, even after twenty years, the sort of magic that Kim Dae-jung worked. The rest of us, we twenty reporters, were simply puppets in his grand scheme.

My dear wife, who is Japanese but is very shrewd on political issues, not least on Korea, said, "You'd better watch out. This is a Kim Dae-jung-led exercise." She said this from the beginning. When I review this now, yes, it was of his making. Kwangju was Kim Dae-jung's political base, but the people there were stomped on viciously by the military, by the armed services. This was not Kim Dae-jung's doing at all, but unfortunately, it was his strategy. It was exactly what he intended. I did not understand that the role of this man could be such from inside prison, a person incarcerated in Seoul.

Kim Dae-jung was saved by associates of Ronald Reagan, who later became the president of the United States. In the fall of 1980, they secretly made an agreement with President Chun Doo-hwan, who was in control of the military. Chun Doo-hwan promised not to execute Kim Dae-jung on the condition that he (Chun) be invited, as the first Korean head of state, to the United States by the newly elected President Ronald Reagan. Reagan pleaded to not have Kim Dae-jung executed because the image of Kim as a leading figure of the democratic movement in Korea prevailed in America.

When the uprising was planned by the supporters of Kim Dae-jung and when Kwangju was occupied, the Western media reported, across the board, that Kim was a "good guy" who promoted democracy. In contrast, the army was the "bad guy." This good-guy bad-guy syndrome lasted for years. We still haven't recovered from it.

Even now in America, Kim Dae-jung is believed to be a hero of the democratic movement in South Korea. But Kim was not a good guy. I regret that I was not aware of this at all. In Kwangju more than 300 people were killed.[1] They were not only civilians, but soldiers as well. Kim Dae-jung should have been called out for responsibility. All of these people surrounding Kim Dae-jung, who instigated the Kwangju Uprising, knew how down-to-earth Kim Dae-jung was, and how avidly he pursued money, status, and power. His purpose in coming to power was to accumulate wealth for his family. People around him knew all of this from the beginning, but they hid these facts from the foreign media.

Regret at Not Having Been Aware of the Facts

But what is more sinful than accumulating wealth was his act of selling his own country, equivalent to treason. I refer, of course, to relations with North Korea. Kim Dae-jung was deeply corrupt. Soon after he became president, a popular joke among ordinary people was that his real name was Kim Dae-ho, meaning money-lover. Korea belongs within the sphere of Chinese civilization, after all. The peninsula is an extension of China on the Asian continent, unlike Japan. Historically, rulers of China and Korea were crazy about embezzlement. Kim Dae-jung was one of those rulers. Posing as a democratic hero of Korea, he made up his mind to get the Nobel Prize for Peace solely for its prestige.

When I first visited South Korea in 1968, the country was still poor. Park Chung-hee built modern Korea. Park was educated during Japanese rule and became an officer of the Japanese Army in Manchuria. He disciplined himself in the rectitude of the Japanese spirit. Making use of the material and spiritual assets Imperial Japan left in Korea, he changed Korea into a modern state in two decades. Had he not been assassinated, he would have attained a lot more.

In the 1960s and 1970s Korea was always next to danger. I was a target of assassination because, as a correspondent, I was writing about things the South Korean administration and army did not want to be reported. The American ambassador to Japan, Mr. Mansfield, proposed that he send a senior staff member as my bodyguard to ensure that nothing happened to me on trips to Korea. I declined his offer. But the embassy received information through the KCIA that plans had been made for me to have an accident, probably an accident on the street. It didn't have to be a knife or pistol. That threat went on for about six months during and after the Kwangju Uprising.

We don't have anything like that today. I don't think there is any Western journalist who is threatened in the way that I was. That's generally true right across society. There was an acidic atmosphere, a sort of toxic atmosphere in the '60s, '70s, and '80s.

A friend always said, "I can't trust Kim Dae-jung. He is in the pocket of North Korea. He's working for the North, not for the South." I rebutted his accusation, saying, "That's ridiculous. He has contributed to the democratization of South Korea. He's Christian, and a sincere and honest man." But I was wrong.

As soon as he was elected president, Kim proved that his government was a puppet of the North. I just regret I hadn't been more aware as a journalist.

2. KIM IL-SUNG AND THE DPRK

Historic Encounter with Kim Il-sung

I had an opportunity to meet Kim Il-sung, who was ordered by the Soviet Union to establish a nation called the Democratic People's Republic of Korea. It was June 1980, immediately after the Kwangju Uprising.

At that point the Americans figured a resumption of war between North and South was likely at any time on the Korean peninsula. They feared that the fighting would be not sporadic, but an all-out war. Under such circumstances, a plan to send a VIP to North Korea was devised and carried out. Its purpose was to clearly inform them that there was no intention of pressuring or waging war against the North. Everything fell into the hands of the United States. It was a difficult task to tell North Korea's head of state that the United States had no intention of restarting war. The question was: who was going to tell him that?

The mission was given to Stephen Solarz, a congressman from New York. It was also decided that a reporter from *The New York Times* would accompany him. *The New York Times* asked its parent company, *The Times of London*, to choose the best person for the job and *The Times* thought I was appropriate. The New York side negotiated with North Korea and I received an invitation. The condition, however, was that I could not attend the meeting between Congressman Solarz and Kim Il-sung. I would be allowed to shake hands with Kim, but not to attend the meeting. I entered North Korea with Solarz. He was always attended by a "minder," perhaps a State Department or CIA agent.

It was the fourth day of our stay. We were told that we were to meet somebody important. I was excited with anticipation. We were taken to Pyongyang Airport and flew to the northeast; we landed at a small airport. We were never told about our location, but we got into a car, drove over several mountains, and finally reached our destination. The place looked like a second home. We drove up a hill and got out of our car in front of a clubhouse-like wooden, one-story house. Then we walked up a hill a little and found a man in a worker's uniform welcoming us. It was Kim Il-sung.

I saw a hump on the back of his neck. He was certainly Kim Il-sung, I thought. Kim greeted Congressman Solarz first, and then he greeted me. A reporter from *Time* magazine and a TV reporter from the American network *NBC* were there, but I represented the media. A young attendant, possibly from the State Department, whispered repeatedly, "No media allowed!" Solarz had been sternly told by the State Department not to let the media report on the meeting with Kim Il-sung.

The New York Times placed my article on the front page, but below the fold, not above it. The message dispatched from America was, "America does its best to prevent war from breaking out." It included mention of American protection of Kim Dae-jung.

I thought it was a historic opportunity, as a reporter. Only a handful of Western reporters were permitted to be there. An American reporter from *The New York Times,* Harrison Salisbury, entered the North in 1971 for the first time as a Western reporter. I was the second. I was the first British reporter.

Truckloads of Political Prisoners

Luckily, I had an opportunity to spend five days in Kim Il-sung's palace in the suburbs of Pyongyang. The palace was like a military version of Versailles. It was on a vast piece of land surrounded by moats, and there were an uncountable number of rooms. The bathroom was 10 or 20 times larger than one you would find in an ordinary hotel. Perfumes collected from all over the world were there, with a variety of different aromas.

We had parties every night while we were in Pyongyang, so I sent an article to New York every night to report on what was going on. Every night at 11 p.m. a limousine arrived in front of the hotel. I took it, alone, to get to the post office to send the article I wrote to New York.

The rest of the time I was with high-ranking North Korean officials. They looked like respectful people. They had dignity and explained North Korea's policy toward America. It was very logical and coherent, so I was deeply impressed. I thought North Korean officials had noble souls. They were totally different from South Korean officials, whose priorities were money and self-interest. North Korean officials were detached from those earthly desires, and told me about their policies, ideals and convictions. They had a spirit of independence.

By contrast, South Korea is heavily dependent on America. North Koreans defend their country, and decide various policies by themselves. In the North, I was unable to feel the sense of dependency which one can readily observe in South Korea and Japan. Gently and calmly, North Korean officials explained various things, which was very impressive. No Western reporter wrote as I did: "I felt dignity from North Korean officials."

I was given an opportunity to do some sightseeing. Sitting with an official in the back seat of our limousine, I observed buildings of various government ministries and large-scale farms. While we were sightseeing I came across, quite by accident, a convoy of about 15 trucks. The trucks were loaded with a lot of men. Instantaneously I learned from the eyes of those men that they were in a miserable situation. Immediately I knew that they had come from a political prison. I was shocked by seeing the reality: the gap between the leaders and the political prisoners in North Korea.

North Korea is a dictatorial state. Its army was under absolute control of its administration. Political prisoners were put into jail and, of course, there was no freedom of speech. I knew I had seen the reality of this country when I saw the eyes of the men carried by trucks. The high-ranking officials were like master poker players. Officials fabricate things every day in order to manage the country. I observed an opera produced by North Korea. The main character, who had a beautiful tenor voice, played a journalist. Every single North Korean production was comical and dramatic.

3. PRINCE NORODOM SIHANOUK IN NORTH KOREA

In North Korea Sihanouk Produces a Film about the Japanese Army

One of the most outstanding leaders in Southeast Asia was Prince Sihanouk. His name, when pronounced in French, lacks the "h" sound but when referred to in English, the "h" is pronounced.

Sihanouk liked art and had lived in Paris. He also regarded politics as an art, which attracted a lot of people. Due to his character, he was loved by everyone inside and outside Japan. The Guinness Book of Records identifies Sihanouk as "the man who has the world's greatest variety of political offices." Certainly he lived a life with ups and downs during the Cold War period in tumultuous Asia.

When he came to the throne in Cambodia under French colonial rule, he was eighteen years old. In March 1945 the Imperial Japanese Army disarmed the French Army. Then Sihanouk declared Cambodia independent. After the Japanese Army's defeat, Sihanouk recognized French rule again, conditionally, but continued to proclaim Cambodian independence in various countries, including America. In 1949 he was recognized for his proclamation of independence within the French Union, but France kept its right to control the police and military. Sihanouk insisted on complete independence and detained himself in the palace. This led to anti-French protests all over the country. In November 1953 France finally recognized Cambodia's independence, and Sihanouk was a focus of respect from all nations as the "father of independence."

In 1955, Sihanouk resigned from his position as king, leaving the position to his father, and became chairman of a political organization. Sihanouk, however, won all seats in the general election and became both prime minister and foreign minister. After his father passed away in 1960, he left the position of king vacant and exercised strong leadership as the head of state.

In March 1970 General Lon Nol, who was at the time both prime minister and defense minister, launched a coup d'etat and dismissed King and Head of State Sihanouk, who was traveling overseas at that time. General Lon Nol changed the name of Cambodia to the Khmer Republic and became president. America supported Lon Nol, as he was pro-America. Sihanouk then established a government-in-exile in China. While in exile he stayed in North Korea as Kim Il-sung's "dinner guest."

When I was invited to Kim Il-sung's palace located in the suburbs of Pyongyang, I accidentally met Prince Sihanouk. The palace was built by Sihanouk for North Korea. At that time America's defeat in the Vietnam War was foreseen as almost certain.

There is a movie entitled *Rose of Bokor*, produced by Sihanouk in 1969. It was shot in a film studio in Pyongyang. It starts with a portrait of Kim Il-sung followed by subtitles praising him. Speeches were all dubbed in Korean. The story starts with a scene of Bokor in Cambodia. All the villagers come out and stand along the street to welcome the advance of the Imperial Japanese Army. Sihanouk plays the role of Colonel Ichiro Hasegawa, the Japanese commander. Princess Monineath takes the part of a daughter of an influential man in town and the colonel's girlfriend. The movie is good evidence of Sihanouk's deeply-felt gratitude towards Japan. The Imperial Japanese Army in the movie is extremely orderly. North Korean People's Army soldiers, mobilized as extras, are cast as Japanese soldiers.

Upon arrival of the Imperial Japanese Army, the local people welcome them as liberators with delight and joy. The French flag is lowered from the headquarters of the French Army and instead, the Japanese national flag, the Hinomaru, is raised while the Japanese national anthem, "Kimigayo," plays. Colonel Hasegawa can be described as a dignified Japanese soldier in his uniform with military sword. The scene in which hundreds of North Korean People's Army soldiers salute the Japanese national flag with their rifles, under the direction of Colonel Hasegawa's sword, is just incredible.

When a French commander dies in a battle between the Japanese and French armies, his funeral is held in a church at the top of a hill. Colonel Hasegawa, who attends the funeral, salutes his enemy. The Japanese officers show sincere respect to enemy officers as well.

On the wall of Colonel Hasegawa's office is a picture of the Emperor in his military uniform, riding a white horse. When the colonel's assistant informs him of the atomic bombing of Hiroshima and leaves, the colonel bursts into tears. When the colonel is officially informed of Japan's surrender, he visits his girlfriend's house in town and plays "Sakura" on the piano. Accompanied by the piano melody, various scenes of Japan are shown in succession: cherry trees in full blossom, mountains and rivers in autumn and trees with leaves of red and yellow, an image of the countryside covered with snow in winter, etc. Sihanouk's message: the beauty and dignity of Japan will never be lost.

Both Kim Il-sung and his son, Kim Jong-Il, showed up for the preview of the movie. Afterwards both of them praised the movie, saying, "It was an excellent piece." I heard about this episode from a close aide to Sihanouk. I also watched the movie, but I am sure both Kim Il-sung and Kim Jong-Il learned how grateful Southeast Asian leaders feel toward Japan.

Sihanouk a Guest in Kim Il-sung's Palace

Sihanouk was like a god to the Cambodian people. He was also known as a playboy in Paris. He played the saxophone at nightclubs in Paris and was known as a superb player. When I met him, I spoke with him in French. Sihanouk, who was born in Phnom Penh in French Indochina, responded by saying, "Monsieur, your French pronunciation is beautiful, but it has a slight Parisian accent." I was fluent in French as I had lived in France, but I did not have the faintest idea that my French had a Parisian accent. Sihanouk was very careful; he mentioned nothing about Kim Il-sung. At that time, America continued its war in Vietnam and carried out indiscriminate bombings against international law.

Sihanouk stayed in Kim Il-sung's palace, where I spent five days. The place was called "Sihanouk Palace." I was with Richard Bernstein of *Time* magazine and a free-lance journalist from NBC TV. As I was a correspondent from *The New York Times,* I was given more respect than anybody else. Sihanouk always welcomed us with a smile.

You might assume that security was extremely tight, but that was not the case. I was not able to spot any security guards anywhere within the palace. It was approximately five kilometers from Pyongyang, on a mountain, but I did not feel any security presence at all. Every night incense was burnt with huge torches, which were lit up when it got dark. I went to the post office by car around 11 p.m. every night to send my article to *The New York Times*. Then, one day, I suddenly noticed a troop of soldiers standing still along the streets coming from the palace entrance. In the darkness I suddenly saw soldiers with rifles standing in the light of my car. In Western countries, at least, they would stand on a platform with lighting even if they had to stand in the dark. It was as if I was in a fantasy world. In such a world lived both Kim Il-sung and Sihanouk.

I was surprised to find that Kim Il-sung was giving the maximum treatment to Sihanouk. I wondered how many friends Kim Il-sung had in the world. Perhaps none. Sihanouk embraced a lonesome Kim Il-sung. Thus Kim Il-sung took extremely good care of Sihanouk, as one would an indispensable friend.

4. SUKARNO, FOUNDING FATHER OF INDONESIA

Meeting Sukarno Immediately after the September 30th Incident

Sukarno, who was respected in Indonesia as the founding father of Indonesia, played a major role in Indonesia's achieving independence. He was from Surabaya, Java. His father was a schoolteacher, and his mother was from an aristocratic family. His name was taken from Karno, a master martial artist, who appear in Java's Anecdote.

In 1927, he organized the People's Party of Indonesia and appealed for Indonesian independence. Thus he was often arrested by the Dutch colonial authorities. In December 1941 the Imperial Japanese Army instantaneously swept the Dutch Army from the Dutch East Indies. Sukarno was released from detention, and thus started cooperation with the Japanese Army for Indonesia's independence.

Only two days after the Japanese surrender, Sukarno, together with Hatta, declared Indonesian independence. Then the Dutch invaded Indonesia again to colonize it. Indonesians, who had learned of the spirit of *merdeka* (independence), and Japanese soldiers who had chosen not to go back to Japan, cooperated and fought against the Dutch Army, finally attaining independence.

Alas, Sukarno then went to the Chinese and came totally under their spell. In 1965 President Sukarno conspired with the Air Force, which was tied to the Communist Party, plotting to make Indonesia a Communist state. He initiated a coup d'état, and killed six high-ranking Army officials. The Army, led by General Suharto, fought back and destroyed the Communist group. This is referred to as the "September 30th Incident." Consequently, the Indonesian Communist Party, which was the largest political force in the region, collapsed. Sukarno was asked to take responsibility for his pro-China approach. When demands for his resignation spread through the Army, he transferred power to Suharto.

I met Sukarno in Jakarta immediately after the September 30th Incident. He was under house arrest. His watchdogs were tense. His guards weren't ordinary male soldiers. They were all females and their beauty was just out of this world.

All Asian heads of state were leading a luxurious lifestyle similar to that seen in movies. Interestingly enough, they all had their own theaters and appreciated the arts, like playboys. They enjoyed their elegant lives, had tremendous money, and were skilled at convincing women to be their mistresses. The scale of the founding fathers' lifestyles was huge. Mao Zedong, for example, enjoyed a gorgeous life, greedily seeking women and consuming splendid servings of Chinese food and alcohol in Zhongnanhai while tens of millions of people were starving to death due to his failed policies.

When I met Sukarno, he was puffing a thick cigar; I was absorbed by its fantastic aroma. I did not know much about Indonesia back then, so I asked him, "Excellency, what on earth is that which you are smoking?" I thought he was smoking marijuana because in Indonesia, marijuana was widely available. Puffing the cigar, which seemed like he had rolled it himself, Sukarno explained, "This is an Indonesian herb cigar called *kretek*. The man who first asked me this same question was Prince Philip, Duke of Edinburgh ." Then he said in a deep, strong voice, "This is the aroma, Mr. Stokes, which stimulated English people to invade the Far East." He added, "This is the aroma. Its supreme smell attracted whites from Europe to Asia. That's the truth of history." Perhaps China was also attracted by this aroma. If Sukarno's left-wing revolution had succeeded, Indonesia would have turned into a Communist state under Chinese control. It's really spine-chilling to think what Japan's fate would have been if such had been realized.

NOTE

1. Wudunn, Sheryl. "The People of Kwangju Recall 1980 Massacre." *The New York Times*. The New York Times, 28 Aug. 1996. Web. 19 Jan. 2016.

Chapter Nine

Memorable People

1. THE JAPANESE AND THE JEWS

Commonalities between the Japanese and the Jews

The Jewish people have been persecuted for many centuries. It was the Jews who executed Jesus Christ. In the New Testament, even Jesus stated, "Ye are of your father the devil, and the lust of your father ye will do."(John, 8:44, King James Version).

The Jewish people do not recognize Jesus Christ as the Messiah. Jews have maintained their traditional ways in an overwhelmingly Christian, European world. The Jewish people have maintained their original lifestyle, even in America. Naturally, the Jewish people have been sacrificed in Christian society. Throughout the Middle Ages, the Jewish people were oppressed. Anti-Semitism in modern British society originated during the height of the Jewish desire to re-establish the state of Israel in Palestine, where the Kingdom of Judah, destroyed around AD 70, had existed.

The reason Adolf Hitler oppressed and then killed Jews was because he wanted to blame the Jewish people for Germany's defeat in WWI. Hitler believed that a Jewish conspiracy caused Germany's defeat. He elaborated his conspiratorial thinking to German officers and soldiers, as well as to the German people, who experienced the pain of defeat in WWI; the German people believed this line of thinking.

Hitler was a devout Christian. Using the pretext of a conspiracy theory, he massacred the exact people who killed Christ. Anti-semitic hatred among non-Jews certainly existed. Such can be observed reading William Shakespeare's "The Merchant of Venice," which featured a Jewish moneylender.

But the view that all Western Christians hate and discriminate against Jews is really an oversimplification. Not all Christians oppressed the Jewish people. Having said that, I will say myself that I have had the feeling that the Jewish people are different from non-Jewish people. I felt that whenever I met with Jews. Such a feeling of difference elsewhere has in fact raised hatred toward Jews.

The Japanese are quite different in this respect in that they treated Jews the same as other people. The Japanese, also, like the Jewish people, have been degraded by Christians. In this respect, the Japanese and the Jews are the same. The rationale behind this is that both races excel. The Japanese were victorious over white Russians in the Russo-Japanese War. In the Greater East Asian War, the Japanese swept away Western colonialism, which had been a fact of life in Asia for several hundred years. After Japan's defeat in WWII, Japan rapidly recovered and created the world's second largest economy. Even today, Japan is still the only non-white nation among the G8 countries. Japan is different from other countries in Asia. The Japanese are an excellent race. They are similar to the Jewish race. Both races are superb, and they are often the envy of the other races, and become the target of criticism.

Hideki Tojo Deserves Recognition for Saving Jews

There is a deep tie between the Japanese people and the Jews. It is well known that Jews were largely responsible for Japan's ability to finance the Russo-Japanese War. No one thought that Japan, a tiny East Asian country, would win a war against the white Russian Empire.

As a Russo-Japanese War became likely, the deputy governor of the Bank of Japan, Korekiyo Takahashi, went overseas with the mission of selling Japanese government bonds to raise money necessary to cover war expenditures. Potential buyers were reluctant. Somehow, Takahashi managed to sell the equivalent of five million pounds in government bonds to bankers, but that was not enough. Under such circumstances, Takahashi attended a house party given by a British banker. At that time, an American sat next to him and inquired about the morale of the Japanese soldiers. As Takahashi was fluent in English, he did his best to explain. Then the following day, the American banker called on Korekiyo Takahashi at his hotel and told him that his bank would accept Japanese national bonds.

This banker was a German-born Jew, Jacob Henry Schiff, who ran Kuhn, Loeb and Co. in New York. Mr. Schiff was an influential banker in the US. He bought the equivalent of five million pounds in Japanese national bonds, and also encouraged Jews all over the world to buy Japanese war bonds. That's how the Japanese managed to finance the war.

Mr. Schiff visited Japan by invitation of the Japanese government. Emperor Meiji awarded him the Grand Cordon of the Rising Sun. At that time, he also dined with His Excellency Emperor Meiji—the very first occasion for a foreign, private individual to receive that honor.

There are many Japanese who know the story of Mr. Schiff. But there is a story not known by many Japanese, let alone by people in other countries. That is the story of how the Japanese saved Jews.

Upon hearing this, you might recall the story of the acting consul of Lithuania, Chiune Sugihara, but the Japanese people I intend to mention are: Major-General Kiichiro Higuchi, who was known as General Higuchi, and Colonel Norihiro Yasue. These two officers have been publicly honored, and their names have been inscribed in the Jewish Golden Book. The Golden Book honors foreigners who have aided the Jewish race. On the cover of Volume 1 is a scene of the sun shining over the city of Jerusalem. The cover is golden, thus the name of the book.

The names of General Higuchi and Colonel Yasue are both found on the 19th Day of Tammuz in the Jewish year 5,701 (July 14, 1941) in Volume 6. But few people realize that the person who should truly be mentioned in the Golden Book is Hideki Tojo.

Toward the end of the 1930s, over 20,000 Jewish refugees were in exile, fleeing oppressive Nazi Germany. They took the Trans-Siberian Railway and reached the border of Manchuria. At that time, Major-General Higuchi was chief of the Kwantung Army's Harbin Special Service Agency. He asked the chief of staff at Kwantung Army Headquarters in Xinjing for permission to issue visas to Jewish refugees. The chief of staff was Lieutenant-General Hideki Tojo. If entry into Manchukuo was not permitted, the Soviets were determined to send the refugees back to Germany.

Tojo, following the Japanese spirit of "the coexistence of five races" and *hakko ichiu* (universal brotherhood), permitted the entry of over 20,000 Jews.[1] The German Foreign Ministry sent a message of strong protest to the Japanese government, but Tojo dismissed German objections, saying that his decision was "the right thing to do from a humanitarian point of view." If Tojo had not given permission then, the Jewish refugees would have perished.

Tojo was the highest-ranking officer involved in this charitable act. His name should have been printed in the Golden Book together with the names of Higuchi and Yasue. But as leaders of the Jewish community in Harbin were not aware of Tojo's role, his name is not listed. Tojo was judged a Class-A war criminal, sentenced to death by hanging, and executed. Tojo is regarded as if he were as monstrous as Hitler. He has been treated unfairly.

Chiune Sugihara won international recognition and respect as the "Japanese Schindler." But Schindler saved Jews for profit. The achievement of

Tojo, saving the lives of over 20,000 Jews for humanitarian reasons, should be known to more Jewish people around the world.

The Man Who United the British and French Rothschilds

The Sulzberger family owns *The New York Times*. They are Jewish. When I first visited my workplace in *The New York Times* headquarters on 43rd Street in Midtown Manhattan, New York, I met three colleagues; we became friends immediately. They were all sharp and intelligent, had excellent senses of humor, and were interesting and attractive, compared with other staff members. They were Jews. Since then, I have found that I get along well with Jewish people.

I am also closely related to a financial conglomerate family. The history of the Rothschild family is astonishing. They are a Jewish family from the northern part of what is today Germany, a family of merchants residing in the Free City of Frankfurt, part of the Holy Roman Empire. Mayer Rothschild started off by selling rare coins in the 1760s, and later became an official merchant for the Earl House Crown Prince Wilhelm of Hesse-Kassel. In 1789 the Rothschild family bank was recognized as an official financial institution of the Hesse-Kassel family. The Rothschilds started their trust-banking business in Germany, servicing all of Europe. After the Napoleonic Wars, the Hesse-Kassel family collapsed. Wilhelm went into exile, but Mayer was appointed his overseer and left to manage his considerable assets. Thanks to help from family members all over Europe, the Rothschilds acquired an enormous amount of wealth. After Mayer Rothschild died in 1812, his five sons started businesses in different countries. The eldest son chose Frankfurt, and the others Vienna, London, Naples and Paris. Each son became influential in his location.

When I became an economics reporter, I sensed that I would meet one of the Rothschild family members someday. They were all in important positions.

In 1963, one year before I brought *The Financial Times* to Tokyo, I was editing overseas news related to the economy at headquarters in London. When my colleague, who was in charge of Europe, was on vacation, I had to do some editing on his behalf. Among those I contacted was Gilbert de Botton, a young banker based in Zurich. I didn't know his background at all, but I thought he might have something to write about. He was a freelance journalist working for *The Financial Times*. He rarely wrote articles and hadn't earned much. I asked, "Will you write something?" He said he would, but he never sent us anything.

A little later I took a vacation in Switzerland and went skiing. De Botton was staying at the luxurious Palace Hotel in St. Moritz. I met him for the first time when we went to the hotel's dance party. He was a small guy with a shining face. We became friends immediately. However, I wondered how de Botton could afford to stay at the most prestigious hotel in Switzerland. He was covering the Rothschild family. The Palace Hotel was the Rothschilds' usual accommodation. At that time, Elie de Rothschild was staying there. He was called *der Elie* by the hotel employees in a very friendly manner.

De Botton made history five years later. Until then, the Rothschilds in London and the Rothschilds in France were on distant terms. They didn't trust each other. The French Rothschild family was the same. De Botton had thought the Rothschilds were one united family. However, they had broken up into five branches, each operating in a different city: London, Paris, Venice, Hamburg and Zurich. De Botton thought it would be wonderful if they were to unite once again.

Engineering a reunion was a big job, but De Botton was a man of action. He established a Rothschild bank in Zurich, and united the Rothschild families in London and Paris. It was de Botton who suggested that I write a book about Yukio Mishima, telling me that I would regret it if I did not. He persuaded me. If he hadn't, I wouldn't have written *The Life and Death of Mishima Yukio*.

The Key to Opening Up a Closed World

One day de Botton phoned me and said, in a rushed manner, "Henry, come to the Plaza Athenee immediately." The Plaza Athénée is the most prestigious hotel. De Botton always used the most prestigious hotels as his stage. "Come over immediately, and bring your Mishima Yukio reference materials," he added. He said, "Come with Akiko (my wife)," and hung up.

My wife and I went to the Plaza Athénée, where de Botton introduced film director Roman Polanski to us. At that time it was just an introduction, but one year later, when we met de Botton, he was managing some of Polanski's assets. Being connected to the Rothschild family, you gain access to various classy European people. De Botton had the key that opened up a tightly-closed door to the world. I was introduced to Polanski when he produced his film *Chinatown*. De Botton was selling the idea of producing a film about Yukio Mishima. But he ended up just having an idea. De Botton had this ability to surprise people.

The phone rang one morning when I was in Paris. A deep voice said, "I am Elia Kazan." I was surprised and asked, "What can I do for you?" The exchange lasted only for about thirty seconds. Kazan, well known by everyone for his film *On the Waterfront*, had phoned me directly. Intuitively, I thought it was about the production of a Yukio Mishima film. Why on earth, however, was a world-famous movie director calling me? Only de Botton could make this happen.

A film about Yukio Mishima was released in 1985. The famous American Paul Schrader was the director. He wrote the screenplay for the film *Taxi Driver*, which was then a major worldwide hit. Schrader paid a sudden visit to the Foreign Correspondents' Club in Japan. He had the screenplay, which he had written himself, with him. George Lucas helped with production, and the film was shot in Japan. When it was released, the title was *Mishima: A Life in Four Chapters*; it failed at the box office.

Jacob Rothschild is a leader of the Rothschild family and is well known in the art world. He is still active. His residence outside London is a work of art. I did not like him because he was arrogant and cold, but he was able to expand his business, thanks to de Botton.

To my young son Harry, de Botton was his godfather. I once accompanied Harry, Jacob and de Botton to Jerusalem. Harry soon got along with the de Botton family. I hope Harry and the children of the de Botton family can do something together. It is advantageous for Japan if our family and the Rothschilds can maintain our relations for future generations.

What It Means to Be a Quaker

The reason I feel empathetic towards Jews and Japanese is perhaps because I am a Quaker. The Quakers are a subset of Christianity. We have always been discriminated against. We cannot be bureaucrats, military personnel, or lawyers. We were not allowed to own land. Such was the background for our seeking a new continent, leaving England and travelling to America. We have sympathy towards the Jewish people who have lost their land.

The Quaker faith was founded by George Fox in the 17th Century. We do not bow to authority. We believe in liberty and independence. Even when we bow, we do not take off our hats. We are known for our sincere attitude and good manners. As Quakers are a minority, we have suffered. So have the Jewish people. The Japanese are the same. They are a minority, so they are hated throughout the world, saddled with claims that they committed massacres or coerced women into sexual slavery.

We Quakers do not have any priests. We gather to meditate, and those who are inspired during meditation stand up and share their thoughts with the rest of us. When we speak a little too long, the elders, in a very moderate tone, suggest that we conclude our speeches. We do not sing hymns. We do not enforce any doctrine. We respect each individual's inspiration. Each person faces his or her own conscience. Our place of assembly is made of wood. There are no luxurious decorations. Such simplicity resembles Japanese Shinto shrines. We do not blindly believe in the Bible. We have faith in Jesus Christ, but we would rather ask ourselves, "What is Jesus Christ?" There is no formality or dogma. I can get along with Jews or Japanese people well because I am a Quaker.

2. FRIENDS WHO INTRODUCED JAPANESE LITERATURE TO THE WORLD

Donald Keene Was Moved by Japanese Soldiers' Noble Spirit

Three individuals, Donald Keene, Edward Seidensticker, and Ivan Morris are well known as foreigners who introduced Japanese literature to the world in the 1950s. They were all good friends of mine. These three people, who translated and introduced Japanese literature to the world, were trained during WWII by the armies of Japan's enemies: America and England.

People think, mistakenly, that I am well versed in Japanese literature. Though I read English translations of Japanese literature, I am not a professor of Japanese literature. I never translated Japanese literature into English. This misunderstanding arises from the fact that I was close to these three men, and that I wrote about Yukio Mishima.

Donald Keene acquired Japanese citizenship in 2012 and his message, "I will live the rest of my life in Japan," was widely reported in Japan. When he had his Book Break at the FCCJ, I acted as moderator. Keene entered Columbia University on a scholarship at the age of 16. He bought a book simply because it was inexpensive, though it contained a great many pages. The book was *The Tale of Genji* by Lady Murasaki, translated by Arthur Waley. It was this encounter which moved him, which inspired him to learn the Japanese language and concentrate on research on Japan.

In 1942, after he earned his undergraduate degree from Columbia University, he joined the US Navy's Japanese language school. It was a total immersion program, which prohibited the use of English. He read Japanese books, wrote papers in Japanese, and spoke only in Japanese all day, even outside of classes. Winning or losing the war hinged on language skills. Even after he was transferred to the front lines, what he faced was life-or-death training. Upon completion of such training, he served as an intelligence officer, interpreting in the Pacific Theater of WWII. He conducted interrogations of Japanese POWs and translated diaries and letters stolen from the bodies of deceased Japanese soldiers. Those diaries and letters were soaked in blood and smelled bad. They were taken from decomposing bodies. The purpose of the translations was to learn the situation of the Japanese Army, to grasp what was advantageous or disadvantageous to the Japanese Army. Keene was moved by the nobleness of the Japanese.

The Japanese Army was completely cut off from supplies. Many soldiers starved to death. Keene saw with his own eyes the Japanese soldiers who fought with superhuman will power. Many of them were less than 20 years old. They fought bravely and died in battlefields far away from their parents and brothers.

Keene says he is a pacifist because of his experiences on battlefields.

Ivan Morris Dedicated *The Nobility of Failure* to Yukio Mishima

Ivan Morris was the person I was closest to among the three, and we had family relationships. Ivan was born in London. His father was an American novelist, Ira Victor Morris, and his mother was a Swedish novelist, Edita Morris. His background was similar to Keene's. He learned Japanese during WWII as a cadet in the British Army. This experience inspired him to extend his study of Japanese culture at Harvard University. He earned his doctorate at the University of London, where he explored the writing style of *The Tale of Genji*.

He was one of the first who visited Hiroshima as an interpreter. Then he worked for the BBC and the Foreign Ministry, and also taught at Columbia University. As a researcher of Japanese literature, he translated *Makura no soshi* by Sei Shonagon. *Sarashina nikki* by the daughter of Sugawara no Takasue, and Ihara Saikaku. Morris also translated Showa-era novels like *Kinkakuji* by Yukio Mishima, *Nobi* by Shohei Ooka, and *Tabiji* by Jiro Osaragi into English.

I met Morris when he was enjoying a comfortable life in New York. Among the three scholars, he was the richest (the other two were far from rich). Translation takes up a lot of time and effort, but the monetary reward is not so great. If you can translate a bestseller like *Harry Potter*, that's another story. But otherwise, it is tough to make a living, so the other two became university professors. Morris had money because his father owned a meat-packing company in Chicago.

Morris decorated everything around him, various belongings, calligraphy, paintings as well as women. One of his many wives was a Japanese woman. Morris died early, at the age of 50. Just before he passed away, he published his last piece, *The Nobility of Failure*. It's a thick book on Japanese heroes; in it he introduces various historical figures. Shoin Yoshida was the quintessential Japanese-style hero. Japanese heroes emerged from failure. *The Nobility of Failure* presents the ultimate image of heroes in Japan. The Japanese hero must maintain his idealism while he suffers defeat. Following his conviction of what is just, the Japanese hero stands on a stage and faces a very strong opponent. While he is defeated following his faith, prestige and praise is raised and encouraged for him. Morris found the beauty of the Japanese in failure.

Morris started writing *The Nobility of Failure* after Yukio Mishima's death in 1970. It does not include a section on Yukio Mishima, but was dedicated to him. Yukio sent a letter to Morris just before his suicide. Morris received the letter immediately after Mishima's death. Mishima made specific plans for the handwritten letter to arrive at Morris's residence at the same time as the news of his suicide.

The Nobility of Failure reserved one chapter for the *Tokkotai* (suicide attack corps). Morris' description is full of deep observation and understanding. *Tokkotai* pilots sacrificed their lives, at the age of sixteen or seventeen, by acting as human bombs, crashing into huge American battleships. Morris accepted their acts in the same way as he did those of other heroes. He saw an image of Japanese beauty and heroism in the manner of *Tokkotai* fighters, sacrificing their lives for a great cause.

Both Keene and Seidensticker were shocked by Mishima's death. It was Morris, however, who felt Mishima's spirit. Such understanding led to the compilation of *The Nobility of Failure*. Morris did not write about Mishima. He just wasn't able to. It was so vivid. *The Nobility of Failure*, written immediately after the Mishima incident, echoes with Yukio's spirit.

These three incredible individuals translated Japanese literature into English so that Japan would not be seen as something mysterious from the outside world. By reading Soseki Natsume's novels, I feel that Japan and the West are not so much different. Human beings are similar, whether they are in the East or in the West. Circumstances and customs may be different, but the Japanese and Westerners are both human.

The preoccupation with determining that the Japanese are atrocious barbarians is wrong. The propaganda about the Japanese, that they rape all women and kill all men on the battlefield, is simply wrong. Westerners must look at the essential part of the Japanese without prejudice.

The role Donald Keene, Edward Seidensticker, and Ivan Morris played was big, in terms of deepening our mutual understanding between Japan and America. The three started translating Japanese literature into English in the '50s. Until then, not so much translation of Japanese literature into English had been done. Arthur Waley translated *The Tale of Genji*, but there were not so many other translators. Waley, in this respect, was the teacher of those three.

Edward Seidensticker is known for his translation of *The Tale of Genji*. He was confident that he was a better translator than Waley, who produced something more or less like a summary, which reflects his own interpretation. Seidensticker focused on being faithful to the original, but such translation is very difficult. If ten different persons translated the work, there would be ten different translations. Translations by the three are masterpiece works.

Morris translated Mishima's *Temple of the Golden Pavilion* (*Kinkakuji*). I think the last forty pages or so are very well translated.

Keene became a naturalized Japanese. Seidensticker sold his condominium in Waikiki, Hawaii and bought one in the place he loved, Yushima in Ueno. He died there at the age of 86. The more the two of them came to know about Japan, the more they fell in love with the Japanese respect for *wa* or harmony, discipline for public-consciousness, and a keen sense of beauty.

The two were more Japanese than the Japanese.

3. MEMORABLE JAPANESE

Introductions to Kazuko Aso and Jiro Shirasu

My mother, Elizabeth Morland, was one of the first group of women allowed to enroll in the University of Oxford. During WWI, she devotedly worked for an institution which took care of orphans, helping them to eat and bathe. After that, she entered Oxford and met my father.

Sir Oscar Morland was my mother's brother-in law. He served as the British ambassador to Japan in the 1960s, and was awarded his honorary knighthood when he assumed that post. He went back to England at just about the time I was assigned to work as the first Tokyo Bureau chief of *The Financial Times*. Sir Oscar Morland was a professional diplomat. He never dealt directly with business or trade, unlike diplomats of the past thirty years. Today diplomacy is a commercial enterprise as well. The job of an ambassador is to expand trade. The yardstick by which to evaluate an embassy is the amount of trade it can generate. In Oscar's days commerce was denigrated.

When I arrived for the first time in Tokyo and stayed at the Hotel Okura, Oscar introduced me to Jiro Shirasu, Kazuko Aso and others. I was a young financial journalist back then, and I was puzzled when an old man introduced me to them. I did not feel any gratitude for this. I was young and did not know how society worked. I did not think the introductions were important. I didn't know how valuable these old people were. I was not aware of the importance of a British ambassador's introducing his relative, a young reporter, to Jiro Shirasu. The same goes for Kazuko Aso. I thought the whole business was troublesome, and never thought of making use of such contacts.

Kazuko Aso, a daughter of Shigeru and Yukiko Yoshida, was born in China. After graduation from Sacred Heart Girls' High School, she extended her study at Sacred Heart Girls' High School in Rome, and then enrolled in the University of London. Due to her mother's influence, she became a devout Christian. She married business owner Tagakichi Aso. Her son is Taro Aso, a former prime minister and incumbent finance minister. Her daughter became Her Excellency Princess Nobuko when she married Prince Tomohito of Prince Mikasa's family. After her mother passed away, Kazuko Aso accompanied her father, Prime Minister Shigeru Yoshida, on his overseas trips as acting first lady. She accompanied him to the San Francisco Peace Conference.

Young Henry Scott-Stokes thought Kazuko was a nuisance, and a meddlesome middle-aged woman. Kazuko took the trouble to rent a house for me. I should have accepted her kindness graciously.

There are many young journalists at the Foreign Correspondents' Club of Japan. They could be better off if they asked for help from someone like me, who has lived in Japan for a long time. But they prefer to do things all by themselves. I insist, though, that it is vital to go through life allowing your-self to be taken care of by your seniors.

Kazuko was noble and attractive. She had the airs of high society. Just as in England, there is high society in Japan. Young Henry Stokes, however, found that writing articles was more productive than attending parties or having a cup of tea with Kazuko. I met Taro Aso several times. One of his close friends, Christopher Purvis, is a good friend of mine. He is chairman of the Japan Society in London.

My Impressions of Jiro Shirasu

Jiro Shirasu was born in 1902. After graduating from Kobe No. 1 High School in 1919, he entered University of Cambridge. As his father's business Shirasu Shoten had gone bankrupt, he returned to Japan upon graduation and became a reporter for the English language newspaper Japan Advertiser. Then, in 1937, he became a member of the board of directors of Nippon Shokuryo Kogyo, later Nippon Suisan. As he frequently traveled overseas, he managed to get to know Shigeru Yoshida, then Japanese ambassador in London. Shirasu used the embassy as his personal place for "regular stays." He was drafted toward the end of the war, but managed to escape the draft, and joined an antiwar group gathering around Shigeru Yoshida.

Upon request by Foreign Minister Yoshida, he became an advisor of the Central Bureau of Communicating the End of War in 1945. Jiro boasted that GHQ called him the "one and only Japanese who is not obedient." In 1948, he became the first director of the Trade Agency. He reformed the Com-merce and Manufacture Ministry, and established the Ministry of Interna-tional Trade and Industry (MITI, the former name of the current METI). In the same year, he tried to sell a Nippon Steel Hirohata factory to a British corporate firm, but was unsuccessful due to opposition from Shigeo Nagano.

In 1950 he traveled to America with Finance Minister Hayato Ikeda (later prime minister) and his secretary Kiichi Miyazawa (later prime minister) to prepare for the peace treaties. In September of the following year, he at-tended the San Francisco Peace Conference as an advisor to the Japanese delegation. He served as an advisor to the Foreign Ministry until September 1954. After that he returned to the business world to become chairman of Tohoku Electric Power Company. After his resignation from Tohoku Elec-tric, he became chairman of Osawa Shokai, and then served as a board member or advisor of Taiyo Gyogyo, Nihon TV and Warburg Securities (currently USB). "I am not a volunteer" was his favorite phrase. He was always after money. By helping British firms to come into the Japan market, he had 5% of the contracts deposited into his bank account in London. Such handsome commissions enabled him to enjoy a luxurious lifestyle till the end of his life.

I didn't like Jiro so much because he was arrogant and boastful at all times. His desire to show off was very strong and he was always boastful. Jiro came in his old black Daimler, a very fashionable automobile, to the Okura Hotel where I had my accommodation. He picked me up, and we went to a very luxurious Japanese-style *ryotei* restaurant. Jiro was handsome like a movie star and spoke impeccable British English. He leaned over and talked as if he were looking down on me. He acted in a rude manner, turning his head in the other direction and ignoring anyone he was not interested in whenever they came close to him. Still, my British friends told me that Jiro was an amazingly well-informed individual.

Jiro often came to Christopher Purvis' office in Uchisaiwai-cho. He valued his relationship with Christopher and regarded him as his British friend, but once he sat down on the sofa he stayed there all day, without any consideration to Christopher's work.

Jiro was chairman of the Golf Club in Karuizawa, and used the facility for socializing. His arrogant attitude never changed there, either. One day, Christopher arrived at the club just five minutes late. Jiro was trembling mad. But nobody was able to stop him; we simply accepted the way he behaved.

I met Jiro on many occasions. I was invited with my wife, Akiko, to a gorgeous lunch at Maxim's de Paris in Ginza. Jiro was a big spender. That was the misery of his life. To enjoy such a life, he was fishing for international business all the time. Jiro was well known among foreigners who dealt with him as a money-chaser and a miser. He was an advisor to British Shell Oil. John Loudon, a big shot in the European business community, acted as go-between. Jiro had many such contacts. He visited those contacts and asked them for financial support. S.G. Warburg gave financial aid to Jiro after Shell Oil resigned. Warburg was Jewish. Warburg once recommended that I become a banker, but I thought it was more fun to work as a journalist. Come to think of it, I would have been able to live much more gracefully if I had become a banker. S.G. Warburg Investment Bank was booming then, but later went bankrupt.

Nobusuke Kishi and Shintaro Abe

For incumbent Premier Shinzo Abe, Nobusuke Kishi was his dear grandfather and Shintaro Abe his father. Former Prime Minister Nobusuke Kishi had his private office in the Nippon Oil Building in Uchisaiwai-cho, about a half mile from the Foreign Correspondents' Club of Japan in Yurakucho. Perhaps Kishi was offered the use of a room in the Nippon Oil Building. That's where I met this historical figure. It was my longtime desire to meet this man, who played a key role in Manchukuo.

Nobusuke Kishi was small and tanned from playing golf. In the corner of his room, I saw a golf bag. Kishi is known as a historical figure, but my impression of him was that of someone who was not fully confident. It was a 45-minute interview. We enjoyed talking, but he never touched on history or politics. I respected the way he brought up topics, as he was in a position which had access to top-secret information. I was happy and honored just being able to meet him. He had a low voice that was not energetic, but he talked calmly with concentration. I was moved by his sincere attitude.

I met Shintaro Abe, the father of the incumbent prime minister, in 1982 when I was Tokyo Bureau chief of *The New York Times*. It was just before Yasuhiro Nakasone was elected prime minister of Japan. Dentsu, the biggest advertising agency in Japan, was in charge of making Shintaro Abe the next premier. One day, a Dentsu man came to see me and asked me to write an article for *The New York Times*.

A one-hour interview was held on a sunny summer day in the garden of Shintaro Abe's residence. We sat in comfortable chairs and talked in a very relaxed manner. The content of our conversation, however, was not satisfactory at all. There was, in fact, no content. Maybe it was because I did not dare to ask more in-depth questions, but still, he told me nothing I was able to use to write an article. I told the New York head office, "There's no way Shintaro Abe can be the next prime minister. He's not good at telling stories."

Several weeks later, I received a phone call from Dentsu. The man on the other end of the line asked, "Have you already sent your article to New York?" So I answered, "No, I even haven't written it. Abe-san told me nothing I was able to write about for an article." The man was definitely not happy. He told me that he wanted me to add some lines to make up a good story. But he was not sure what I should write, so I was unable to add anything. Of course, I did not want to make up a story purely out of my imagination. Such a thing just can't be done.

Fortune Smiles on Yasuhiro Nakasone

By contrast, Yasuhiro Nakasone was lucky. Together he, US President Ronald Reagan, and British Prime Minister Margaret Thatcher moved the world in the '80s. His presence as a world leader was strong in a transitional period in world history. The three made the Soviet Union, the headquarters of socialism and communism, which divided the world in half against the Free World, disappear. They did not expect, perhaps, to accomplish that, but they did, with a fair amount of luck factored in.

I first met Nakasone in 1968 at a symposium in Shimoda. Mike Mansfield, who later became US ambassador to Japan, was also there. I was with Nakasone at a buffet-style dinner. Since then, we've met often at different places. He was a young conservative politician yet to hold a ministerial position. He became Defense Agency chief in 1970, the year Yukio Mishima died. Nakasone became influential thereafter, and people expected him to assume much more important positions. He held a press conference at the Foreign Correspondents' Club of Japan the year following Mishima's death. I interviewed him after he became prime minister. I was a *New York Times* reporter, and was with two reporters from other news media. I did not propose an exclusive interview to him. I was biased against Nakasone, so I did not want to support him by conducting an exclusive *New York Times* interview.

However, the three big shots (President Reagan, Prime Minister Thatcher and Prime Minister Nakasone) were at the pinnacle of international politics at an historic phase, as the socialists' global power started to collapse. It was the end of the Cold War, a period of tension between the US and the Soviet Union. America had been defeated in the Vietnam War. It was predicted that America's power would gradually diminish. In the '70s the winds favored the leftists, and the world was overwhelmed by socialist expansion, with the Soviets at its pinnacle. In the '80s, however, the wind blew in a totally opposite direction.

Once Reagan, Thatcher and Nakasone appeared as leaders of the free world, the world changed. The three behaved as if they had made the global transition. They acted accordingly and got the wind of the time behind them and let things continue to roll. In Poland Walesa led Solidarity, which he co-founded; a non-communist leader suddenly took leadership of the country's labor unions.

In 1989 the Berlin Wall collapsed, and everything started changing at an aggressive speed. Neither President Reagan nor Prime Minister Thatcher could have imagined that the Soviet Union would simply disappear. Nakasone, in this respect, was a lucky man. With such luck, he did his job. The wind of the time blew, and it was behind Nakasone. The timing by which he became Prime Minister, the fact that his administration lasted for six years, and his developing a close relationship with Ronald Reagan (called the "Ron-Yasu" friendship) all indicated that Nakasone had strong luck.

NOTE

1. Tokayer, Marvin, and Mary Swartz. *The Fugu Plan: The Untold Story of the Japanese and the Jews during World War II.* New York: Paddington, 1979. Print.

暗躍する国際共産主義.PNG

暗躍する国際共産主義。
日本に仕掛けられた謀略工作。
支那事変は国と国の戦いではなかった！

映画「南京の真実 支那事変と中国共産党」は、映画「南京の真実 第一部 七人の死刑囚」に続く、汚された祖国日本と祖先の名誉を取り戻そうとする映画である。の歴史捏造を暴き出し、事実に基づき、

「南京大虐殺」は、連合国の極東軍事裁判（東京裁判）において、突如、提起されたともない歴史捏造「事件」である。支那事変において、南京攻略戦という戦争があり、支那将介石軍側に多数の戦死者は出たが、民間人も含め「虐殺」など一切無かった。本当にあったのは、東京大空襲や広島長崎への原爆投下による日本人数十万人の大虐殺である。それを隠そうとする連合国側の歴史捏造プロパガンダだけが、南京攻略戦に至る歴史事実を日本の国内外に知らしめるようとする映画作品である。

この作品は、支那事変に関する膨大な映像資料や文献を集約し、検証し、

映画は第五部まで続く予定だが、本映画は支那大陸の清帝国滅亡から、辛亥革命、張作霖爆殺、満州事変、盧溝橋事件勃発までを描いており、映画として世界で初めて明らかにされる歴史事実が数多く出てくる。多くの観客は衝撃を受けるだろうと思う。ひとつ例を挙げれば、支那事変はドイツが仕組み、蒋介石政権を支援して起こし、ナチス時代になっても、その姿勢は変わらなかった。そして、そのナチスドイツを育て、支援したのは、アメリカの石油メジャーや国際金融資本だったということである。連合国側映画はその驚くべきを事実を会社名や人名を明らかにしながら、日本軍国主義の暴走と侵略という捏造プロパガンダを事実に基づいて、木っ端微塵に粉砕していく。

もう一つ、明らかにされるのは、中国共産党政権の真実の姿である。観客はこれにも衝撃を受けるだろう。中国共産党政権は、1949年の建国以来、国内の民だけでも七千万人以上を「殺して」来た。そして、日本を除く周辺諸国ほぼ全てと戦争や武力紛争を行ってきた。映画はその実態を暴き、「南京大虐殺」という歴史捏造プロパガンダが、単なる反日政策ではないことを明らかにしていく。

映画「南京の真実」の製作と上映は、単なる映画制作ではない。戦後七十一年続いてきた「戦後レジーム」に対する日本からの反撃である。それも、これまで行われてきた「慰安婦」や「南京大虐殺」の歴史捏造に対する日本国民はそんなに悪いことはやっていない、という反撃に対する反撃とどまらない。逆に反転攻勢として、「悪いのはお前たちだったじゃないか」と、その悪行と企みの歴史事実を暴露し、彼らにそれを突きつける映画である。つまり、戦後体制の嘘を歓露と歌諭を批判し、否定するだけではなく、その「正体」を明らかにして、国内外の戦後体制を破壊、溶解させていく強力な武器「黒船」となる映画である。

Chapter Ten

People of Japan, Take Pride in Your History

WHY KOREA WILL NEVER CATCH UP WITH JAPAN

Japan annexed Korea in 1910, five years after Japan's victory in the Russo-Japanese War. Japan expended huge sums of money and enormous effort in order to modernize Korea. Those expenditures built the foundation of today's Korean society, encompassing the establishment of an educational system ranging from compulsory to university education, and of medical, police, and military systems. Unlike British colonial rule, Japan spent its own tax money to invest in the building of Korea.

My understanding is that the Korean people accepted such Japanese efforts. Japanese rule was different from Western colonial rule, which was based on racial supremacy. Korean people were treated as if they were Japanese. If we look at British colonial rule of India, the whites were superior to the Indians, of course. Not only in India but in all of Asia, colored people were regarded as inferior beings, compared with the white race.

Education for people in British colonies was forbidden and simply was not offered. Japan, however, built imperial universities in Korea and Taiwan. In the vast British colonies, there was not even one university built for colored people. Even now, the former Japanese imperial universities in Korea and Taiwan are the highest educational institutions in their countries: Seoul University and Taiwan University.

Recently South Korea has become very critical of Japan due to anti-Japanese education. When I was reporting on South Korea, all the Korean people I met adored Japan and hoped South Koreans would grow up respecting Japan as their master. Business owners all looked at Japan as their model. Lee Kun-hee, chairman of Samsung Group, was one of them. Lee and I are

111

friends of over forty years. He is about my age, and is still active as the chairman of Samsung Group. Lee and his father led the business world of South Korea. Both of them were graduates of Japan's Waseda University. All the top leaders of the South Korean business community adore Japan.

There are many areas in which Japan and South Korea can pursue friendly exchanges: pop culture, pop music, fashion, etc. Even in the current anti-Japanese mood, there have been no major protests in central Seoul. We can spot only a few, small demonstrations by professional activists. That is the reality. It is likewise with the comfort women issue.

South Korea developed in the field of electronics and communication. Korea has surpassed Japan's sales in those areas, and South Koreans have become much more arrogant nowadays.

The comfort women issue is complete nonsense. I don't understand why the comfort women became such a major topic. They are simply used as a propaganda tool to establish an "evil Japan" image. In Korea, there were many comfort women for the UN Forces, mostly organized by American forces. The Korean government used to issue special IDs for women who dealt with Japanese men on their "sex tours." Those women were earning foreign currency so they could freely go in and out of hotels.

Of course, South Korea is gaining power, but the major countries in Asia are Japan, China and India. Japan and South Korea should be the most familiar nations. South Koreans will never catch up with the Japanese unless they develop good relations with Japan. To hide their inferiority complex, Koreans criticize Japan to satisfy their psychological well-being. But the more they do that, as complex such a negative feeling is, the more negative the results will be. Eventually, they will lose an important asset called Japan.

However, this twisted relationship between Japan and Korea was originally caused by the Japanese, who are too modest and overly degrade themselves. Japan has the longest unbroken dynasty in the history of the world. Japan has its own history the Japanese people can very proud of. Nonetheless, the independent spirit that once came naturally to the Japanese seems to have been lost due to the American invasion and the Occupation.

50 YEARS OF DISPATCHING NEWS FROM TOKYO

I am a dear son of newspaper. For over fifty years I have been in service, and I witnessed the fall of the newspaper world. In 2013 Amazon, an Internet sales firm only twenty years since foundation, took over *The Washington Post*, a prestigious newspaper which has over 140 proud years of history. When Katharine Graham, the owner of *The Washington Post*, visited Japan in the 1980s, the entire Japanese political and business community welcomed her, and she behaved like an American queen.

On October 2013, the Japan Newspaper Association held its convention, which attracted 500 executives of newspaper companies. They all talked about what they could do to halt the decline of readership, which translates into the newly-coined newspaper-industry term *mudokuka* in Japanese. In the Japanese market, the number of consumers who do not read newspapers has suddenly expanded.

I have been a Tokyo correspondent and a member of the Foreign Correspondents' Club of Japan since 1964, when the Olympic Games were last held in Tokyo. I am still active, and I am the only one who has been active for over half a century.

The Financial Times is a wonderful newspaper that focuses on economics. The quality of *The Financial Times* surpasses all the rest of the world's newspapers. *The Financial Times*, the pink paper, earned prestige from finance, the economy to art. When I was 20 years old and a student at Oxford University, I read *The Financial Times* for the first time and was astonished. It was far superior to any other newspaper that I had read. And I felt that way every single day. The encounter with *The Financial Times* made me think that I would like to be a journalist, possibly as a team member of *The Financial Times*. I joined *The Financial Times* after I graduated from university. Although I was a novice, I was immediately given a big responsibility. I was assigned to the newsroom, into which news from all over the world was coming at every single moment. Four people including myself worked in the newsroom. I was, perhaps, 23. In the newsroom, we selected which items would be news and which would not. We looked at the events going on in the world at that time, and decided which ones were important. There were twenty five correspondents dispatched around the world working under me. I was given authority to decide which one of the news stories these correspondents were to send me from various parts of the world, how much space *The Financial Times* should spare for a particular news item, and whether to use photos. Such things were all decided at the Head Office in London. All my colleagues were British. We divided the entire world into four areas. I was in charge of Asia, Africa and Latin America. This was such precious experience.

Eventually, I was dispatched overseas as a correspondent. It was *The Financial Times*' policy to have young reporters see the world with their own eyes. I was dispatched to Tunisia, Africa, and Portugal. In Portugal I covered ministers from various countries who attended an international conference held there. I interviewed Edward Hughes, who later became British prime minister. A young man from the English countryside was with Hughes, then a British minister. A young man who had never had the experience of living in a city like London now had access to high society.

Although I started my career as a journalist, my ability did not particularly surpass other reporters. I just devoted myself to my assignments. Then one day, I was told to go to Tokyo and was dispatched from the London head-quarters. This was my fate, come to think of it. I have stayed in Tokyo for over half a century since then as a Tokyo correspondent. I started out with *The Financial Times*, then I became the Tokyo correspondent of *The Economist*, the Tokyo Bureau chief of *The Times* of London and then of America's *The New York Times*. I have reported news to the world from Tokyo.

One thing all journalists should keep in mind is that media like TV or newspapers has enormous power. Real journalists and ad-agency professionals know that from experience.

With a simple report on TV, let's say about a new product or a new company, we can create an image in the minds of consumers. Let's take a new medicine as an example, how people can judge an effect of a medicine nobody has ever tried. The influence of the media, including advertisement, is so huge. That is why so much money is spent on publicity. I joined the world of media attracted by news reporting, the power of influence, impacting all of society. But it is so difficult to report the truth. We have to be very careful. It is said that democracy is run by arrogant journalists and cowardly politicians. Among politicians, Shintaro Ishihara is the only one in Japan who can scold the media head-on.

THE DEFEATIST SYNDROME
AND THE JAPANESE CONSTITUTION

In an editorial, an editor of a major South Korean newspaper wrote that the dropping of atomic bombs on Japan was the price of sin Japan had to pay. That was an unacceptable remark. America has also justified the atomic bombing of Japan. But their justification, that the atomic bombings ended the war much earlier and saved the lives of many people, is a lie. The atomic bombing was not at all necessary to end the war sooner.

There is a puzzling thing on the Japanese side, too. Why does a country upon which atomic bombs were dropped have to pledge, "We will never make mistakes again?" It is America that must apologize, not Japan. Ben Bruce Blakeney was an American lawyer who served as a major in WWII. At the Tokyo Trials, he defended Shigenori Togo and others. He argued that an aggressive war could not be defined as a crime under international law. He further argued that "if the killing of Admiral Kidd by the bombing of the Pearl Harbor is murder, we know the name of the very man whose hands loosed the atomic bomb on Hiroshima." He further mentioned that he could state the names of the commander and the president of the country which dropped the atomic bombs. The point he made was that if Japan was going to be punished, America had to be punished as well. Therefore, the court was not just; it was simply seeking one-sided revenge. America, however, has never apologized to Japan for its atomic bombardment.

Before the US Senate's Foreign Relations Committee, MacArthur said, "The [purpose of the Japanese], therefore, in going to war was largely dictated by security." In other words, in testifying that Japan waged a war of self-defense, MacArthur himself was admitting that the Tokyo Trials were not just. MacArthur realized, after he fought the Korean War, that Japan had fought a war of self-defense. He noticed that the Japanese argument was correct.

Germany apologized at a very early stage. In other words, the Germans apologized immediately after WWII, and started their postwar era. So we have the argument: why couldn't Japan handle the issue as Germany did? But Germany's Hitler waged a war of aggression, aiming to place all of Europe under his rule. Japan was different. Japanese authorities did their best to avoid going to war with America, but America wanted a war to break out, and provoked Japan to strike America first. Japan was a cornered rat, so to speak. The Japanese were forced to wage a war of self-defense to protect their own country and their own people. As MacArthur said, they waged a war because their own security was at stake. Why is it necessary for Japan to apologize?

In Germany's case, the sins Hitler committed against Jews were obvious, so it was easier for Germans to apologize. Thus, the Nuremberg Trials ended immediately. The Japanese had experienced their first defeat in history. They just didn't know how to accept such a reality. But it has been almost seventy years since the end of the war, so the Japanese people should overcome their defeatist syndrome.

The original draft of the Japanese Constitution was written in English. It was prepared by the General Headquarters of the Occupation army. An occupying army forcing an occupied country to change its constitution is against international law, but GHQ wrote the draft of the Japanese Constitution and forced Japan to accept it. MacArthur produced the draft of the Japanese Constitution in only one week. Among the staff members who drafted the constitution, there was no one who specialized in constitutions. They composed the draft referring to documents such as the UN Charter. The Constitution of Japan is a treaty of surrender. It is obvious from its Preamble that the Allies' intent was to make Japan a country which can never again wage war against America.

Among the drafters was a young German-Jewish woman who had no background in law. Her family came to Japan, saved from Nazi oppression by Japan. Her parents were musicians. She was assigned to write articles related to women's rights. Beate Sirota Gordon, despite her moral debt to Japan, proudly talked about her achievement well into old age. What she did to Japan was to destroy its culture-based lifestyle and replace it with something shallow. There's no country in the world where women are better treated than Japan. The fact that Japanese women, on average, have the world's longest life span proves it. Beate Sirota Gordon fawned to GHQ and claimed that women were being abused by men in Japan, a lie.

Recently in Japan, there has been a boom of books on the Japanese Constitution. There are many books about the Japanese Constitution on the shelves of bookstores. The Japanese Constitution is called the "Pacifist Constitution" by the Japanese, but if you read the Preamble to the Constitution carefully, you will realize that it is a protectorate treaty. It obliges the Japanese to leave the survival of their people in the hands of America.

The fetter for Japan which does not allow a change in the protectorate position is Article 96, which requires a vote of at least two-thirds of Diet members for amendment of the Constitution. What Yukio Mishima appealed for in exchange for his life was: If Japan discards its soul and remains America's mercenary, Japan will no longer be Japan. Japan cannot be independent as long as it protects a constitution illegally forced on it by the occupying army during the Occupation period.

Japan should have an original constitution, one based on Japan's own history and traditions and its own national forces. Japan cannot become an independent state without these. Many Japanese people believe it is possible, but this is not true at all.

INCONVENIENT TRUTH FOR THE WEST: HISTORICAL VIEWS BASED ON "THE GREATER EAST ASIAN WAR"

This year (2013) commemorates the 70th anniversary of the Greater East Asiatic Conference held in Tokyo in 1943. I have already mentioned the significance of this conference in Chapter Seven. The Western nations labelled the Greater East Asiatic Conference an assembly of puppet governments under occupation by Japan. But it is a historical truth that the leaders of independent colored nations (whose independence was attainable only when Japan won the fight against the colonial powers) gathered together in Tokyo. India attended the conference only as an observer because at that time it had not declared its independence. Chandra Bose participated in the conference as head of the Provisional Government of Free India, which sought complete independence. Malaya and Indonesia were not able to attend because they had not declared independence. Indonesia intended to become independent in September 1945.

People believe the Japanese Army invaded Asia. Why on earth, then, did the leaders of those Asian countries gather together in Japan, the country which invaded Asia? Unless those leaders were empathetically in favor of the purpose of the war Japan was fighting, they wouldn't have gathered together.

The spirit of independence from Western colonial rule, with the help of Japan, became strong among the people of Asian countries. This cannot be understood as long as we have the perception that Japan invaded Asian countries. We won't be able to see the truth. Independence of Asian countries from Western colonial rule was only achievable by Japanese military advancement. This is a solemn fact.

Japan, under unjust pressure from America, could have merely waged war against America. But, at the same time, Japan raised the idea of liberating Asia from Western colonial rule. The Meiji Restoration took place to protect Japan from colonial rule by Western imperialism. The liberation of Asia was an extension of the Meiji Restoration.

At first the Western powers did not understand what was going on, but gradually it became clear that various Asian colored races were determined to stand up and fight for their independence. If Japan had not advanced into Asia, those countries might still be colonies of the West. Moreover, in America there's no chance that a black man could become president. Rather, black people are still suffering in their miserable positions in society.

As Japan fought the Greater East Asian War, the British Empire collapsed. If Japan hadn't made military advances, Britain, France, Holland and America would still control Asia. The Pacific Theater wasn't the only battlefield for Japan. The Western colonies were spread all over Asia. Why is Japan's war called the "Pacific War?" The theater was all the Western colonies spread over East Asia. Japan did not name its war the "Pacific War."

In order to understand the true reason why Japan fought in such a vast theater, we must adopt the historical viewpoint of the Greater East Asian War, which turned Greater Asia into Japan's theater of war, fought against Western colonial rulers who robbed Asians, and eventually liberated Asia. It is entirely damaging for America and European colonial rulers if history is seen from the viewpoint of the Greater East Asian War, because such a view will make it clear that it was Western colonial rulers who exploited Asia, not the Japanese. Therefore, it is advantageous for white people to record history as Japan's having fought a "Pacific War."

If it were known that Japan's contributions were made with the aim of independence for Asian nations, then the atrocious actions of white people in Asia would become obvious. Justice as window-dressing would collapse. If the historical view of the Greater East Asian War is asserted, the Western colonial rulers' basis for war will collapse and brought to light will be the fact that it was the Western powers which invaded Asia.

The reason Japanese views are not well understood overseas is that Japan hasn't made an effective appeal to international society. One of the critical reasons is that such efforts haven't been made in English. On the contrary, apologetic statements such as those made by Kono or Murayama have been issued. Such behavior has totally the opposite effect.

PRIME MINISTER ABE AND JAPAN'S FUTURE

Compared with his father Shintaro Abe, incumbent Prime Minister Shinzo Abe is much more persuasive. The same person became Japanese prime minister twice for the first time since Shigeru Yoshida. Shinzo Abe has a very different style from his father and grandfather. Moreover, Shinzo Abe is a very lucky man.

Napoleon said, "Whether a general has luck or not determines everything." Abe is supported by the public. Of course, those opposing his politics are anxiously waiting for his failure. But so far, Abe hasn't failed. He is still winning vast support.

My son, Harry Sugiyama (Sugiyama is his mother's maiden name), has daily TV shows on Fuji TV (Channel 8) and NHK (National Broadcasting, Channel 1), as well as an FM radio program on J-Wave. He recently wrote about himself in *Number 1 Shimbun*, the Foreign Correspondents' Club of Japan's monthly magazine for club members. In his essay (written in English) he expressed his support for Prime Minister Abe. This is proof that many Japanese youths have a good impression of the prime minister.

When I interviewed Prime Minister Abe's father, Shintaro Abe, the headquarters of *The New York Times* did not expect him to be the next prime minister. Yasuhiro Nakasone, who had strong leadership, came into attention as the next prime minister.

Prime Minister Shinzo Abe is full of stories. Luck is with him, so he won the right to host the 2020 Olympic Games in Tokyo. His appeal is clear, providing a lot of source material for media coverage. I feel that he speaks from conviction, in his own words. The First Lady, Akie Abe, is very lively. Abe is popular because he lets his wife be free in her speeches and actions. The couple is very different from the traditional Mr. and Mrs. Prime Minister, so they are very interesting. One of Abe's lucky factors is his wife, who has a very personable presence.

Princess Hisako of the Takamado Family gave an excellent speech at the IOC Assembly in Buenos Aires, urging that the 2020 Olympics be held in Tokyo. When the decision was announced, I sent her a congratulatory e-mail. Until now, no imperial family member has had the opportunity to participate in such an event. The Imperial Household Agency opposed Princess Hisako's participation, claiming the imperial family was being used for political purposes. Nonetheless, approval was granted because the request emanated from the Cabinet. The sight of Prime Minister Abe, together with an imperial family member, giving final presentations on Tokyo's behalf, gave us a strong impression of "All Japan."

Prime Minister Shinzo Abe won the right to host the 2020 Olympics in Tokyo, increased GDP figures, and raised the consumption tax rate. He is gradually satisfying conditions enough to be called a great prime minister.

The fact that the 2020 Olympics will be held in Tokyo means that stable economic growth for the next six years seems to be guaranteed. This kind of opportunity comes once in a long time. My son Harry repeatedly said, "Thank God." Harry has just started his own small firm, so he must have honestly felt so.

Shinzo Abe has proclaimed he will end the postwar regime. If the social system established during the Occupation continues, Japan will lose its strength and disappear from international society. Politicians and novelists live in totally different circumstances. However, Abe's aims and the spirit of Yukio Mishima have some common ground.

Index

Profile: Henry Scott Stokes

Henry Scott Stokes was born in England in 1938. After earning an undergraduate degree from Oxford University in 1961, he joined the Financial Times, Inc. He became its first Tokyo branch representative in 1964. He became Tokyo Bureau Chief of *The Times* in 1967 and became Tokyo Bureau Chief of *The New York Times* in 1978. He is known as the most intimate friend of Mishima Yukio among foreign reporters in Japan. Immediately after Mishima's death, he wrote *The Life and Death of Yukio Mishima* (Farrar, Straus and Giroux Inc., New York).

Added to this, he has worked extensively in the arts. For almost a decade after leaving *The New York Times* in 1984, he worked with New York artists Christo and Jeanne-Claude on a joint work of art for Japan and America titled "The Umbrellas." During the l990s he worked for several years for Mary Moore, the daughter of British sculptor Henry Moore. Thereafter in the 2000s and 2010s he served as a writer, editor and lecturer on a range of interests.

Henry Stokes was raised in an atmosphere shaped by his Quaker mother's pacifism and his father's eclectic interests, who served as an army officer in two world wars, a scholar of both Winchester College and New College Oxford and a lifelong businessman heading a shoe business. He is married to Akiko Sugiyama and they have one son Harry, who is engaged in TV and radio work in Tokyo.